T0349021

Security and Privacy for Modern Networks

Strategies and Insights for Safeguarding Digital Infrastructures

Seshagirirao Lekkala
Priyanka Gurijala

Apress®

Security and Privacy for Modern Networks: Strategies and Insights for Safeguarding Digital Infrastructures

Seshagirirao Lekkala
Milpitas, CA, USA

Priyanka Gurijala
Milpitas, CA, USA

ISBN-13 (pbk): 979-8-8688-0822-7
https://doi.org/10.1007/979-8-8688-0823-4

ISBN-13 (electronic): 979-8-8688-0823-4

Managing Director, Apress Media LLC: Welmoed Spahr
Acquisitions Editor: Susan McDermott
Editorial Project Manager: Jessica Vakili

Cover image designed by Freepik (www.freepik.com)

Distributed to the book trade worldwide by Springer Science+Business Media New York, 1 New York Plaza, Suite 4600, New York, NY 10004-1562, USA. Phone 1-800-SPRINGER, fax (201) 348-4505, e-mail orders-ny@springer-sbm.com, or visit www.springeronline.com. Apress Media, LLC is a California LLC and the sole member (owner) is Springer Science + Business Media Finance Inc (SSBM Finance Inc). SSBM Finance Inc is a **Delaware** corporation.

For information on translations, please e-mail booktranslations@springernature.com; for reprint, paperback, or audio rights, please e-mail bookpermissions@springernature.com.

Apress titles may be purchased in bulk for academic, corporate, or promotional use. eBook versions and licenses are also available for most titles. For more information, reference our Print and eBook Bulk Sales web page at http://www.apress.com/bulk-sales.

Any source code or other supplementary material referenced by the author in this book is available to readers on GitHub. For more detailed information, please visit https://www.apress.com/gp/services/source-code.

If disposing of this product, please recycle the paper

Gratitude to the pioneers of Security and Privacy for Modern Networks. Your insights have illuminated the path in Strategies and Insights for Safeguarding Digital Infrastructures. Your dedication to safeguarding information is instrumental in shaping a secure digital future.

Table of Contents

About the Authors

 **Seshagirirao Lekkala**, a seasoned cloud and network security expert, brings a potent combination of an Electrical and Electronics Engineering degree with 16 years of robust experience in architecting software solutions for the telecommunications industry. Renowned for his expertise in engineering highly scalable, distributed networking solutions tailored for cloud and AI technologies, his strategic insights and architectural ingenuity have been critical in generating multibillion-dollar revenue for industry giants. His groundbreaking inventions in SD-WAN and adaptive traffic engineering established him as a leading figure in the field.

His commitment extends beyond technical mastery; he actively fosters the professional development of emerging talent through mentorship and contributes to the industry's body of knowledge through his scholarly articles. His influence is acknowledged in both academic and professional spheres, as he frequently serves as a judge at various national and international events, including startup pitches and hackathons. This underscores his reputation as a reliable and distinguished leader in network security.

ABOUT THE AUTHORS

 **Priyanka Gurijala**, with over a decade of experience, is a recognized expert in designing robust cloud networking solutions. Holding a master's degree in Electrical and Computer Engineering from the University of Maryland, College Park, she has played pivotal roles in driving product success and fostering organizational growth at industry-leading companies. Currently at the forefront of innovation, she applies her expertise in networking and artificial intelligence to advance Azure cloud infrastructure capabilities. She has made significant contributions in the fields of secure network configuration and remote management. She excels in translating visionary concepts into practical solutions, rigorously evaluating functionality, and refining technologies to align with industry standards, demonstrating her steadfast commitment to technological progress.

About the Technical Reviewer

 **Raghavaiah Avula** is a seasoned telecommunications and cloud security professional with over 18 years of experience. Currently a Senior Principal Software Engineer and Senior Architect at Palo Alto Networks, he excels in designing and implementing innovative solutions such as the SASE Multitenant Platform and 5G security systems. Raghavaiah has a robust background in wireless technologies and cloud-driven SaaS solutions. He holds multiple patents, including Private Wireless Network Guest Access, System and Method to Facilitate Hotspot Onboarding for User Equipment in a Network, Environment Forming Channel Device Groups within a Citizens Broadband Radio Service Band. His expertise and leadership in the industry are complemented by his active role as a judge for various award committees like Globee Awards, Stevie Awards, and QS Reimagine Education Awards recognizing excellence in technology and business.

Introduction

Security and Privacy for Modern Networks illuminates the path to solid cybersecurity and provides a comprehensive toolkit for dealing with today's sophisticated threats. This book delves into the complexities of securing today's digital communication systems, starting with an examination of their evolution and the critical security and privacy issues that modern networks face. The book emphasizes the role of cybersecurity in safeguarding personal, corporate, and national interests, offering both theoretical insights and practical solutions. It covers network security principles, multilayered defense strategies, vital security protocols, and an in-depth understanding of the cyber threat landscape, including threat categorization, attack vector recognition, threat actor profiling, and emphasis on social engineering tactics.

The text explores cryptography as the foundation of secure communications, modern authentication techniques, and the nuances of securing wired and wireless networks. Readers are helped to design secure network architectures, implement defense-in-depth strategies, and ensure data security. It also covers intrusion detection, VPNs, SDN/SD-WAN, and strong perimeter defense. As cloud computing and mobile devices become more common, the book offers strategies for securing these environments while emphasizing the transformative role of AI and machine learning in improving threat detection and data analysis.

Engaging case studies demonstrate real-world applications of the discussed strategies, and a forward-looking chapter prepares readers for future technological shifts such as IoT security and quantum computing. The book concludes with a synthesis of critical security strategies, reflections on the state of network communication security, and a look ahead to evolving cybersecurity paradigms. Additional resources and a glossary provide further learning opportunities, making this an essential guide for anyone committed to protecting modern networks. This comprehensive approach ensures that readers are well-prepared to address both current and future cybersecurity challenges effectively.

CHAPTER 1

Introduction to Modern Network Systems

In the modern era, our lives are becoming more intertwined with complex networks. This chapter serves as a road map for navigating the ever-changing digital communication landscape. We'll start by tracing the evolution of digital communication, emphasizing the advances that have led to the interconnected world we live in today.

"As we navigate the complexities of modern network systems, we must remember that security is a journey that requires constant vigilance and adaptation. We can stay ahead of adversaries and protect our interconnected world by implementing proactive measures such as strong authentication and intrusion detection."

Although the interconnectedness fostered by modern digital technologies has numerous advantages, it also poses inherent security risks. This chapter delves into the changing threat landscape, looking at the increasing sophistication of cyberattacks, the expanding attack surface of the Internet of Things (IoT), and the complex legal landscape governing data privacy and security. However, security is only one aspect of the digital landscape. The chapter also discusses the critical issue of

S. Lekkala and P. Gurijala, *Security and Privacy for Modern Networks*, https://doi.org/10.1007/979-8-8688-0823-4_1

user privacy in the digital age. We investigate the massive amount of personal data collected online, strike a delicate balance between security requirements and individual privacy concerns, and emphasize the importance of user awareness in protecting themselves online. Finally, the chapter establishes the foundation for creating secure and private networks. We cover essential security and privacy principles, essential network security controls, and design best practices, emphasizing the importance of implementing strong user access controls. By the end of this chapter, you will have the knowledge to navigate the complexities of modern networks and understand the importance of security and privacy in the digital age.

1.1 The Evolving Landscape of Digital Communication

The desire to communicate over long distances has existed for millennia. Early forms of communication included smoke signals, drum beats, and visual displays such as fire beacons. Although ingenious, these methods had limitations in terms of range, speed, and capacity. Writing was invented around 3500 BCE, marking a significant turning point. Clay tablets, papyrus scrolls, and later the printing press revolutionized information transmission, but physical transportation remained necessary.

The modern digital communication landscape is a tapestry woven from countless threads of innovation. This section delves into the historical narrative, examining how we came to the point of hyperconnectivity that characterizes our modern world. We'll take a journey through the evolution of communication technologies, highlighting key advancements that transformed information exchange.

1.1.1 From Humble Beginnings: The Dawn of Communication

Our story begins with the early visionaries who laid the groundwork for modern communication technologies. We'll look at the fundamental inventions that sparked a revolution in information exchange, including

- **The Humble Spark – the Rise of Telegraphy (Early 1800s):** Prior to the telegraph, long-distance communication was based on physical message delivery or primitive signaling methods such as smoke signals. The invention of the telegraph in the early 19th century marked a watershed moment. This ingenious device used electricity to transmit coded messages over wires, resulting in the first long-distance electrical communication. The telegraph revolutionized communication by significantly reducing the time required to send messages over long distances.

- **A Conversation Across Wires – the Telephone (1876):** While the telegraph allowed for the rapid transmission of information, it was unable to convey the human voice. In 1876, Alexander Graham Bell introduced his groundbreaking invention, the telephone. This revolutionary device forever changed communication by allowing for real-time voice conversations over long distances. The telephone brought about a new era of interpersonal communication, fostering closer connections and revolutionizing business practices.

1.1.2 The Rise of Networking: Connecting Devices and Sharing Resources

The 20th century saw a paradigm shift away from point-to-point communication and toward interconnected networks. This section delves into key advancements that enabled communication among multiple devices and revolutionized resource sharing:

- **Breaking Down Barriers – the Development of Packet Switching (1960s):** Prior to packet switching, data was transmitted via dedicated circuits, limiting efficiency and scalability. The advent of packet switching in the 1960s was a game changer. This innovation helped in breaking down large data files to smaller packets, allowing for more efficient network transmission. Packets could travel independently, using the most efficient route, and then be reassembled at the receiving end. This breakthrough paved the way for faster and more efficient communication, laying the groundwork for the Internet we know today.

- **A Global Tapestry – the Birth of the Internet (1960s):** The ARPANET project, launched in the 1960s by the US Department of Defense, marked the beginning of the Internet. This project aimed to build a communication network that could withstand disruptions, including during wartime. ARPANET paved the way for the Internet, a global network of interconnected networks that transformed communication and information sharing. The Internet's decentralized architecture enabled scalability and resilience, promoting global collaboration and innovation.

1.1.3 The Mobile Revolution and the Era of Ubiquitous Connectivity

The latter part of the 20th century and the beginning of the 21st century witnessed a mobile revolution that fundamentally altered how we connect. This section looks at the rise of wireless communication technologies and their impact:

- **Untethered Communication – the Rise of Mobile Computing:** The invention of cellular networks and Wi-Fi technologies ushered in a new era of mobile communication. The introduction of smartphones and tablets in the late 20th and early 21st centuries accelerated this revolution. These mobile devices allowed users to access information and communicate from almost anywhere, resulting in a paradigm shift in how we work, socialize, and consume entertainment.

- **A World of Connected Devices – the Internet of Things (IoT):** The proliferation of interconnected devices has caused an exponential expansion in the digital communication landscape, ushering in the Internet of Things (IoT). Countless devices now have Internet connectivity, including smart home appliances like refrigerators and thermostats as well as wearable technology like fitness trackers and smartwatches. This interconnectedness enables data collection, automation, and remote control, transforming many aspects of our lives.

By delving into this historical timeline, we gain a better understanding of the remarkable advancements that have led us to a world in which information flows freely and connectivity is nearly ubiquitous. However, as we will see in the following sections of this chapter, this interconnectedness creates new security and privacy challenges that require our continued vigilance and innovation.

1.2 Understanding Current Security and Privacy Challenges

The interconnectedness facilitated by modern digital communication technologies has undoubtedly improved our lives. However, this connectivity poses a complex challenge: ensuring the security and privacy of our data in a constantly changing threat environment. This section delves into the critical security and privacy issues that require continuous monitoring and proactive measures.

1.2.1 The Escalating Threat Landscape: Evolving Cyberattacks

Cybercriminals are a constant threat to the digital world, developing new and sophisticated attack methods on a daily basis. Here's a closer look at some of the common threats:

- **Malware on the Rise:** Malicious software, which includes viruses, worms, ransomware, and spyware, remains a major threat. These programs are capable of stealing data, causing system damage, or disrupting critical operations. Attackers are constantly changing their tactics and creating new malware variants to get around traditional security measures.

- **Social Engineering – Exploiting Human Vulnerabilities:** Cybercriminals often use social engineering techniques to trick users into disclosing sensitive information or clicking on malicious links. Phishing emails, pretext calls, and social media scams are common tactics that exploit human trust and inattention.

- **Evolving Attack Surfaces – the Challenge of the IoT:** The growing number of interconnected devices in the Internet of Things (IoT) provides a massive attack surface for malicious actors. These devices may have limited security capabilities, making them vulnerable to exploitation and potentially serving as gateways for attackers to infiltrate larger networks.

1.2.2 The Data Deluge: Balancing Security and Privacy

The interconnected nature of modern networks has resulted in exponential data generation and collection. This raises critical questions about balancing security needs and individual privacy concerns.

- **Data Collection Concerns:** A vast amount of personal data is collected online, ranging from browsing history and search queries to social media interactions and location information. While some data collection is required for personalized services and targeted advertising, it also raises concerns about user privacy and the possibility of misuse of this information.

- **The Ever-Changing Regulatory Landscape:**
  Regulatory frameworks for data privacy and security
  are constantly evolving. Businesses and individuals
  must navigate a complex regulatory landscape,
  including the General Data Protection Regulation
  (GDPR) in Europe and the California Consumer
  Privacy Act (CCPA) in the United States.

- **Striking a Balance:** Implementing strong security
  measures is critical for protecting sensitive data from
  unauthorized access. However, this must be balanced
  with user privacy and giving individuals control over
  their personal information.

1.2.3 User Awareness and Education: A Crucial Defense

Security and privacy are more than just technical issues; they also require
user awareness and responsible behavior. This section highlights the
significance of user education:

- **Phishing Awareness and Best Practices:** It is critical to
  educate users on how to recognize and avoid phishing
  attempts. Educating users on how to recognize
  suspicious emails and links, as well as the importance
  of strong password management, can help to reduce
  the risk of successful cyberattacks.

- **Understanding Privacy Settings and Data Sharing:**
  Many online platforms provide privacy settings that give
  users control over how their data is collected and shared.
  Educating users about these settings allows them to make
  more informed decisions about their online privacy.

- **Staying Informed and Adapting Practices:** The cybersecurity threat landscape is constantly changing. Encouraging users to stay informed about emerging threats and adjust their online behavior accordingly is critical for maintaining a strong security posture.

To summarize, navigating the modern digital landscape necessitates a multifaceted approach to security and privacy. We can work toward a more secure and privacy-conscious digital future by acknowledging the constant threats, understanding the challenges of data collection, and increasing user awareness. This chapter lays the groundwork for subsequent chapters that will delve deeper into these critical topics.

1.3 The Critical Role of Cybersecurity in Today's World

In the modern, hyperconnected world, cybersecurity is no longer an option; it is a necessary component of a functioning digital society. Our personal information, financial data, critical infrastructure, and even national security are becoming increasingly intertwined with sophisticated digital networks. This section delves into the critical role that cybersecurity plays in protecting these valuable assets from cyber threats.

1.3.1 Protecting Sensitive Data and Infrastructure

The digital realm contains a vast amount of sensitive data, including personal information, financial transactions, and intellectual property. Cybersecurity measures are necessary for

- **Safeguarding Personal Information:** Data breaches can compromise sensitive personal information such as social security numbers, credit card information, and medical records. Robust cybersecurity helps to protect this information from unauthorized access, theft, or misuse.

- **Ensuring Financial Stability:** Cyberattacks on financial institutions, ecommerce platforms, and online payment systems can have disastrous consequences. Cybersecurity protects financial transactions and sensitive financial data.

- **Maintaining Critical Infrastructure Security:** Our reliance on interconnected infrastructure, such as power grids, transportation systems, and communication networks, necessitates effective cybersecurity measures. Cyberattacks on this infrastructure could cause widespread disruptions and pose national security risks.

1.3.2 Fostering Trust and Confidence in the Digital World

A safe digital environment is critical for increasing trust and confidence in online activities. This includes

- **Ecommerce Security:** When purchasing online, consumers must be satisfied that their financial and personal information is secure. Effective cybersecurity measures increase trust in ecommerce platforms and promote online transactions.

- **Privacy and Data Protection:** Individuals have the right to privacy and control over their personal information. Cybersecurity procedures that prioritize data protection and user privacy are critical to establishing confidence in the digital world.

- **Maintaining Business Continuity:** Cyberattacks can disrupt business operations and cause severe financial losses. Implementing strong cybersecurity safeguards can reduce these risks and promote business continuity.

1.3.3 Promoting Innovation and Economic Growth

A secure and trusted digital environment promotes innovation and economic success. Here's how:

- **Enabling Secure Online Collaboration:** Cybersecurity enables secure online cooperation and communication, allowing businesses to function more efficiently in a globalized world.

- **Protecting Intellectual Property:** Cybersecurity protects valuable intellectual property from theft or unauthorized access, which promotes innovation and research.

- **Supporting the Growth of the Digital Economy:** A safe digital infrastructure is critical to the expansion of the digital economy, which includes ecommerce, online services, and other Internet-based activities.

Prioritizing and investing in cybersecurity allows us to create a safer and more secure digital environment for individuals, businesses, and society as a whole. This commitment to cybersecurity is more than just a technical problem; it is a necessary step in ensuring a prosperous and secure digital future.

This chapter has demonstrated the crucial importance of cybersecurity in today's environment. The following chapters of this book will go into greater detail about establishing a solid basis for security and privacy in modern networks.

CHAPTER 2

Building Blocks of Network Security

The interconnected world provides numerous opportunities, but it also creates vulnerabilities. This chapter provides you with the necessary knowledge to build a strong defense against cyber threats. We'll look at the fundamental principles of network security, the effectiveness of layered defense strategies, and the significance of security protocols and compliance standards.

2.1 Core Principles of Network Security: Anchoring Your Network

In a world where everything is interconnected, protecting our networks is critical. This section establishes the fundamental principles that form the bedrock of network security, laying the groundwork for a strong defense against cyber threats.

© The Editor(s) (if applicable) and The Author(s), under exclusive license to APress Media, LLC, part of Springer Nature 2024
S. Lekkala and P. Gurijala, *Security and Privacy for Modern Networks*,
https://doi.org/10.1007/979-8-8688-0823-4_2

2.1.1 The CIA Triad: Confidentiality, Integrity, and Availability

The CIA triad is a cornerstone of network security, comprising three core principles:

- **Confidentiality:** This principle protects sensitive information by requiring only authorized users to access it. Encryption is essential for maintaining confidentiality. Encryption techniques scramble data into an unreadable format, making it inaccessible to anyone who lacks the decryption key. Common encryption methods include Secure Sockets Layer (SSL)/Transport Layer Security (TLS) for Internet communication and disk encryption for data at rest on storage devices.

- **Integrity:** This principle ensures that data is unaltered during transmission or storage. Data integrity measures such as checksums and digital signatures aid in detecting unauthorized changes. Checksums involve generating a mathematical value that represents the original data. Any changes to the data produce a different checksum value, alerting security personnel to a possible tampering attempt. Digital signatures go a step further by verifying the data's origin and preventing unauthorized changes.

- **Availability:** This principle guarantees that authorized users have access to information and resources when necessary. Network security solutions must strike a balance between defending against threats and keeping the system available to legitimate users. Implementing effective security measures may result in access limits or temporary service outages. It is critical to strike the correct balance between mitigating security concerns and preventing legal network usage from being impeded.

2.1.2 Beyond the CIA Triad: Authentication and Authorization

While the CIA triad serves as the core of network security, two additional principles further strengthen defenses:

- **Authentication:** This principle authenticates the identity of users or devices attempting to access a network or resource. Strong authentication measures are necessary to prevent illegal access. Usernames and passwords are popular authentication methods; however, they can be susceptible. Multifactor authentication (MFA) strengthens security by requiring users to submit additional verification factors, such as a code from a mobile app or a fingerprint scan, in addition to their password.

- **Authorization:** This principle governs access to network resources based on user roles and permissions. Authorization determines which actions users can take within a system. For example, a user with a basic account may only be able to read certain files, whereas an administrator may be able to create, modify, and remove files. Granular authorization rules reduce security risks by limiting user access to only the resources required to complete their job duties.

By following these fundamental principles, you build the framework for a safe network environment. These principles serve as a framework for implementing security measures, influencing decisions regarding access controls, data encryption methodologies, and overall network security posture. The following sections of this chapter will look at how these ideas are turned into real security tactics that are implemented using layered defenses and adherence to security protocols and compliance standards.

2.2 Building a Fortified Wall: Implementing Multilayered Defense Strategies

The ever-evolving world of cyber threats needs a comprehensive strategy to network security. A single security mechanism, no matter how strong, may be insufficient to prevent sophisticated attacks. This section emphasizes the value of a layered defensive system, in which multiple security controls collaborate to form a stronger protection perimeter. Consider a well-fortified castle, with each layer offering another defense against intruders. In the context of network security, these layers operate together to considerably minimize the possibility of a successful cyberattack.

2.2.1 The First Line of Defense: Perimeter Security

Firewalls serve as the first line of defense in a layered security strategy. These hardware or software-based systems act as gatekeepers, thoroughly inspecting every incoming and outgoing communication on a network. Firewalls are built on predetermined security rules that govern which traffic is permitted and which is prohibited. Let's take a closer look at how firewalls protect your network.

- **Traffic Filtering:** Firewalls examine each data packet entering or leaving the network, checking information such as source and destination IP addresses, ports, and protocols in use. Based on specified security criteria, the firewall allows valid traffic to pass while blocking suspicious or malicious traffic attempting to breach the network. A firewall, for example, can be set to block incoming traffic from known malicious IP addresses or to prevent access to specific websites that are deemed risky.

- **Denial-of-Service (DoS) Protection:** Firewalls can assist prevent denial-of-service attacks, in which attackers flood a network with traffic, making it unavailable to legitimate users. Firewalls can detect and filter unusual traffic patterns associated with DoS attacks, protecting network resources and assuring uninterrupted access for authorized users.

While firewalls are an important first line of security, they are not flawless. More sophisticated attacks may be capable of bypassing firewalls. This is why a multilayered protection approach is critical.

2.2.2 Dividing and Conquering: Network Segmentation

Network segmentation divides a network into smaller, more manageable portions. This method can considerably reduce the potential impact from a security breach. Consider a huge palace with several sections. If one portion is penetrated, the attacker's access is limited to that specific location, reducing the overall damage on the network. Here's how network segmentation improves security:

- **Limiting Lateral Movement:** By segmenting the network, you build obstacles that limit an attacker's ability to move laterally within it. If an attacker compromises a certain segment, their access is limited to the resources contained within that segment. This makes it more difficult for them to access vital systems and data on other secure areas of the network.

- **Improved Threat Containment:** Network segmentation enables the installation of more granular security policies on an individual segment basis. This allows you to customize security measures to meet the unique demands of each section. For example, a segment with very sensitive financial data may have greater security restrictions than a section with public-facing web servers. In the event of a breach, segmentation can assist isolate the vulnerable area, preventing the attack from spreading to other key parts of the network.

Network segmentation provides an additional layer of defense by compartmentalizing the network and reducing the possible impact of a security compromise. The section that follows will look at additional security rules that can help build a strong layered defense plan.

2.3 Unifying the Defense: Adopting Security Protocols and Compliance Standards

In the ongoing war against cyber dangers, security measures and compliance standards act as a unifying force. These aspects establish a common vocabulary and a set of best practices for establishing successful network security measures. Consider these blueprints for creating a safe network foundation.

2.3.1 The Power of Protocols: Securing Communication Channels

Security protocols define a collection of rules and principles for ensuring secure communication between devices and systems. These protocols specify how data is encrypted, authenticated, and transported via networks. Here are two popular security protocols:

- **Secure Sockets Layer (SSL)/Transport Layer Security (TLS):** These protocols serve as the foundation for secure Internet communication. SSL/TLS encrypt connection between web browsers and servers, ensuring secure data transmission. When you see a padlock symbol in your web browser's address bar and "https" instead of "http" in the URL, it means that the website uses SSL/TLS to encrypt communication. This encryption assures that even if data is intercepted by attackers, it will be unintelligible without the decryption key.

- **Secure Shell (SSH):** This protocol enables safe remote access to computer systems. SSH encrypts all communication between a client machine and a remote server, safeguarding user passwords and data transfers from unauthorized access. This is especially critical for system administrators who have to handle servers remotely.

By following these and other security protocols, you can ensure that communication channels are encrypted and protected, significantly lowering the risk of data breaches and unauthorized access.

2.3.2 The Importance of Compliance: Aligning with Security Standards

Compliance standards specify security requirements for organizations in specific industries. These standards help to establish a baseline level of data security and reduce the risks associated with data breaches. Here are two major compliance standards:

- **Payment Card Industry Data Security Standard (PCI DSS):** This standard is applicable to organizations that handle credit card information. The PCI DSS requires a set of controls that protect cardholder data from unauthorized access, use, disclosure, alteration, or destruction. Organizations that accept online payments or process credit card transactions must comply with the PCI DSS.

- **Health Insurance Portability and Accountability Act (HIPAA):** This regulation affects healthcare providers, health plans, and healthcare clearinghouses that handle protected health information (PHI). HIPAA requires safeguards to maintain the confidentiality, integrity, and availability of PHI. Compliance with HIPAA is critical for healthcare organizations seeking to protect sensitive patient data.

Understanding and adhering to relevant compliance standards demonstrates your commitment to data security while also mitigating legal risks associated with data breaches. These standards provide a framework for implementing security controls and best practices, ensuring that your organization has a strong security posture.

Understanding the fundamental principles of network security, implementing a layered defense strategy, and adhering to security protocols and compliance standards are all significant steps toward creating a robust and secure network environment. However, the cyber threat landscape is constantly changing. The upcoming chapters will provide you with the knowledge you need to investigate specific security tools and strategies, allowing you to strengthen your network defenses and stay ahead of emerging threats.

CHAPTER 3

Navigating the Cyber Threat Landscape

The continuously evolving landscape of cyber threats can be overwhelming. This chapter will provide you with the knowledge you need to navigate this complex terrain. We'll look at different types of cyber threats and how they exploit vulnerabilities in your network. We will investigate cyber attackers' motivations and tactics. You'll also learn how to identify and mitigate vulnerabilities, as well as how attackers use social engineering to manipulate users.

3.1 Categorizing Cyber Threats and Recognizing Attack Vectors: Understanding the Adversary's Arsenal

The ever-expanding world of cyber threats can be overwhelming, but understanding the various types of attacks and how they infiltrate your network is an important first step toward defense. This section looks at the most common cyber threats and the attack vectors they use to gain access to your systems and data.

© The Editor(s) (if applicable) and The Author(s), under exclusive license to APress Media, LLC, part of Springer Nature 2024
S. Lekkala and P. Gurijala, *Security and Privacy for Modern Networks*, https://doi.org/10.1007/979-8-8688-0823-4_3

3.1.1 Demystifying the Threat Landscape: A Look at Common Cyber Threats

Here's a breakdown of some of the most common cyber threats you'll face:

- **Malware:** Malicious software includes viruses, worms, Trojan horses, spyware, and ransomware. Malware can disrupt operations, steal data, install backdoors to allow continued access, and even hold your data hostage for ransom.

- **Phishing Attacks:** These deceptive attempts trick users into clicking malicious links or downloading infected attachments. Phishing emails frequently impersonate legitimate sources, such as banks, credit card companies, or even coworkers, tricking users into disclosing sensitive information or downloading malware.

- **Denial-of-Service (DoS) Attacks:** These attacks flood a website or server with traffic, rendering it inaccessible to legitimate users. DoS attacks can disrupt business operations, result in financial losses, and harm a company's reputation.

- **Man-in-the-Middle (MitM) Attacks:** Attackers put themselves between a user and a legitimate server, intercepting communication and possibly stealing sensitive data such as login credentials or financial information. MitM attacks can take place on unsecured Wi-Fi networks or via compromised systems.

- **Data Breaches:** A data breach is defined as the unauthorized access or disclosure of sensitive data, such as customer records, financial information, or intellectual property. Data breaches can have serious legal and financial consequences for organizations.

- **Zero-Day Attacks:** These are novel attacks that take advantage of previously unknown vulnerabilities in software or systems. Because there is no patch available, zero-day attacks can be especially dangerous until a security fix is developed.

3.1.2 Recognizing Attack Vectors: How Threats Exploit Weaknesses

Cyber threats do not appear out of thin air. They take advantage of vulnerabilities in your network infrastructure, software, or even human behavior. Here are some common attack vectors you should be aware of:

- **Unpatched Software:** Outdated software with known vulnerabilities provides an easily exploitable entry point for attackers. Maintaining a secure environment requires regular patching of software and systems.

- **Weak Passwords:** Simple or easily guessed passwords present a low barrier for attackers. Enforcing strong password policies and using multifactor authentication significantly reduces the risk of unauthorized access.

- **Phishing Susceptibility:** Employees who are unaware of social engineering tactics are more susceptible to phishing attempts. Security awareness training is critical for informing users about these deceptive practices.

- **Unsecured Wi-Fi Networks:** Connecting to unsecured Wi-Fi networks exposes your devices and data to possible eavesdropping or MitM attacks. It is best to avoid sensitive transactions on public Wi-Fi and instead use a VPN (Virtual Private Network) for extra security.

- **Misconfigured Systems:** Improperly configured systems or network devices can introduce security flaws that attackers can exploit. Following security best practices and configuration guidelines is critical for mitigating these risks.

Understanding the various types of cyber threats and the attack vectors they use enables you to take proactive steps to strengthen your defenses and create a more secure network environment. The following sections of this chapter will delve deeper into threat actors' motivations, discuss vulnerability assessment and risk mitigation strategies, and shed light on attackers' social engineering tactics.

3.2 Profiling Threat Actors and Exploring Their Incentives: Understanding the Why Behind the Attack

The cyber threat landscape is not a single entity. Cyberattacks are orchestrated by various actors, each with their own motivations and skill sets. Understanding these threat actors and their motivations is critical for anticipating their tactics and prioritizing your defensive strategies. This section examines the profiles of some of the most common cyber adversaries:

3.2.1 Unmasking the Attackers: A Look at Different Threat Actors

The motivations for cyberattacks can vary from financial gain to political disruption. Here's a breakdown of some prominent threat actors and their motivations:

- **Cybercriminals:** Driven by financial gain, cybercriminals are frequently highly skilled individuals or organized groups who target both businesses and individuals. They may steal financial information, carry out ransomware attacks, or engage in data breaches in order to sell stolen information on the dark web.

- **State-Sponsored Hackers:** These attackers have the support of a nation state. Their motivations could include espionage, theft of intellectual property, disruption of critical infrastructure, or political influence. State-sponsored attacks are often sophisticated and well-funded.

- **Hacktivists:** Hacktivists launch cyberattacks to disrupt operations, deface websites, or send a message, often for social or political reasons. Hacktivist attacks may target government agencies, corporations, or organizations that they believe are acting contrary to their beliefs.

- **Insider Threats:** Disgruntled employees, contractors, or even business partners with legitimate access can pose a significant security risk. Insider threats can steal data, sabotage systems, or sell confidential information to external attackers.

3.2.2 What Makes Them Tick? Exploring the Incentives Behind Cyberattacks

Understanding the motivations of these threat actors allows you to anticipate their targets and preferred attack methods. Let's take a closer look at some common incentives.

- **Financial Gain:** For cybercriminals, financial gain is the primary motivator. They may steal credit card information, conduct ransomware attacks to extort money, or exploit financial system vulnerabilities for personal gain.

- **Espionage:** State-sponsored hackers frequently target sensitive data, intellectual property, or government secrets in order to gain a competitive advantage or disrupt another country's operations.

- **Disruption and Influence:** Hacktivists use cyberattacks to disrupt operations, raise awareness of their cause, or sway public opinion on a specific issue.

- **Disgruntled Employees:** Insider threats could be motivated by revenge, financial gain, or a sense of injustice. They may use their authorized access to steal data, damage systems, or cause disruptions in operations.

3.2.3 Understanding Their Motivations: A Key to Effective Defense

By profiling threat actors and investigating their motivations, you can prioritize your security measures based on the likelihood of a particular attack type. Understanding the "why" behind an attack allows you to focus your defenses on the most critical vulnerabilities and implement targeted security controls to reduce risks. The following section will look at vulnerability assessment and risk mitigation strategies to help you deal with these threats proactively.

3.3 Strategies for Vulnerability Assessment and Risk Mitigation: Building a Proactive Defense

One ounce of prevention equals a pound of cure. This adage is true in the field of cybersecurity. Proactive vulnerability assessment and risk mitigation are critical for protecting your network and data. This section describes how to identify vulnerabilities before they are exploited by attackers, as well as how to prioritize risks and implement effective mitigation measures.

3.3.1 Unearthing the Weak Spots: Vulnerability Assessment Techniques

The first step toward a secure network is to identify vulnerabilities in your systems and infrastructure. Here are some important vulnerability assessment techniques:

- **Security Scans:** Automated tools will scan your systems and networks for known vulnerabilities. These scans can detect outdated software, incorrect configurations, and insufficient security settings.

- **Penetration Testing (Pen Testing):** Ethical hackers simulate real-world attacks to uncover security flaws in your systems and network defenses. Pen testing assesses the effectiveness of your security controls and identifies vulnerabilities that automated scanners may miss.

- **Vulnerability Management Programs:** A well-defined vulnerability management program includes ongoing scanning, prioritizing identified vulnerabilities, and promptly patching them. This proactive approach ensures that vulnerabilities are addressed before attackers exploit them.

3.3.2 Prioritizing Threats: A Risk-Based Approach

Not all vulnerabilities present the same threat. A risk-based approach allows you to prioritize vulnerabilities according to their severity, likelihood of exploitation, and potential impact. When assessing risk, consider the following factors:

- **Severity:** This is the potential damage caused by exploiting a vulnerability. Data breaches, system outages, and the loss of sensitive information all have varying levels of severity.

- **Likelihood of Exploitation:** Consider the prevalence of attacks targeting this specific vulnerability and the attacker's capabilities.

- **Impact:** Assess the potential impact of a successful attack on your company's operations, reputation, and financial well-being.

Analyzing these factors allows you to prioritize vulnerabilities and effectively allocate resources to address the most critical risks first.

3.3.3 Mitigating the Risks: Implementing Effective Countermeasures

Once vulnerabilities have been identified and prioritized, it is time to put mitigation strategies into action. Here are some commonly used approaches:

- **Patch Management:** Regularly patching software and systems with the most recent security updates is critical for addressing known vulnerabilities. Patching quickly reduces the window of opportunity for attackers to exploit these vulnerabilities.

- **Configuration Hardening:** This entails reviewing and adjusting system configurations to meet security best practices. Configuration hardening techniques include disabling unnecessary features, implementing strong password policies, and limiting user privileges.

- **Network Segmentation:** Divide your network into smaller segments to reduce the potential impact of a security breach. By isolating critical resources, you can prevent attackers from gaining access to your entire network even if they compromise just one segment.

- **Security Awareness Training:** Educating users on cyber threats and best practices is a critical line of defense. Employees can benefit from training programs that teach them how to identify phishing attempts, avoid suspicious links and attachments, and understand the value of strong passwords and multifactor authentication.

3.3.4 Building a Culture of Security: Continuous Monitoring and Improvement

Vulnerability assessment and risk mitigation are continual activities. New vulnerabilities are continuously identified, and attackers' strategies develop. Stay ahead of potential threats and maintain a strong defense by constantly monitoring your network for suspicious activity, implementing security information and event management (SIEM) tools, and analyzing your security posture on a regular basis.

The following part will look at the social engineering strategies utilized by attackers. While technical security measures are critical, knowing how attackers abuse human psychology is equally necessary for developing an overall security plan.

3.4 Social Engineering Tactics Used by Attackers: The Human Factor in Cybercrime

Technical security controls are an important line of defense, but hackers recognize that the human factor can be the weakest link in any security system. Social engineering strategies leverage human psychology, emotions, and trust to trick people into disclosing sensitive information, clicking dangerous links, or providing illegal access. This section sheds light on these deceptive methods, preparing you to recognize and oppose them.

3.4.1 The Art of Deception: Common Social Engineering Techniques

Attackers use a range of social engineering strategies to manipulate their victims. Here are some of the most common ones:

- **Phishing:** Deceptive emails or SMS messages posing as reputable sources, such as banks, credit card firms, or even colleagues. Phishing emails frequently instill a sense of urgency or anxiety in users, luring them into clicking dangerous links or downloading infected attachments that can steal information or install malware.

- **Pretexting:** Attackers create a situation or pretense to earn your trust and obtain sensitive information. They may impersonate customer service agents, police enforcement officers, or IT support workers to persuade you to disclose sensitive information or grant remote access to your system.

- **Baiting:** This strategy entices customers with a desirable incentive, such as a free gift, prize, or special offer. The lure frequently carries a hidden cost, such as installing malware disguised as a free software program or following a link to a phishing website.

- **Quid Pro Quo:** This strategy provides something in exchange for a favor. Attackers may offer technical assistance or access to restricted information in return for login credentials or system access.

- **Tailgating:** This physical security breach entails following someone who has permitted access to a secure place. Attackers may hold the door open or pretend to have forgotten their access card in order to gain unwanted admission.

3.4.2 Recognizing the Signs: How to Spot Social Engineering Attempts

Here are some red signs to look for while receiving strange communication:

- **A Sense of Urgency:** Phishing emails frequently encourage you to act right away, instilling panic and clouding your judgment.

- **Suspicious Links and Attachments:** Avoid clicking on links or downloading attachments from unfamiliar senders or emails that have grammatical problems or strange layout.

- **Unrealistic Offers:** If something sounds too good to be true, it probably is. Don't give in to the allure of free prizes or exclusive deals that require you to provide personal information.

- **Verification Requests:** Legitimate firms rarely ask for critical information by email or text message. If you're hesitant, contact the sender directly via a verified phone number or website to validate the request's validity.

3.4.3 Defending Yourself Against Social Engineering

Understanding these strategies and taking a cautious approach can considerably lower your chances of falling victim to social engineering attempts. Here are some strategies to strengthen your defenses:

- **Be Skeptical:** Do not automatically trust unsolicited emails, phone calls, or messages. Before responding or clicking on any links, verify the sender's identity and the legitimacy of the request.

- **Think Before You Click:** Hover over links to see the destination URL before clicking. Be aware of abbreviated URLs that hide the actual location.

- **Strong Passwords and MFA:** Create strong and unique passwords for all of your accounts. Enable multifactor authentication (MFA) whenever possible to offer an extra layer of security.

- **Security Awareness Training:** Regular security awareness training can teach users about social engineering techniques and best practices for safe online activity.

- **Report Suspicious Activity:** If you suspect a phishing effort or social engineering attack, notify the proper authorities or your IT security staff.

Staying aware and knowing the social engineering strategies used by attackers can help you protect yourself and your organization from cyber dangers. This finishes Chapter 3, which provided you with the knowledge needed to navigate the cyber threat scenario. The chapters that follow will go into greater detail on various security tactics and technologies that you may use to develop a comprehensive network security plan.

CHAPTER 4

Cryptography: The Backbone of Secure Communications

The digital world is based on the secure exchange of information. This chapter goes into the fascinating area of cryptography, which is essential for preserving data secrecy, integrity, and authenticity in our online interactions. This chapter looks at the various cryptographic techniques that are used to safeguard sensitive data during transmission and storage over networks. We'll look at how cryptography enhances network protection techniques, evaluate advanced encryption algorithms and their different applications, and go over best practices for successful key management and the development of robust cryptographic frameworks. Understanding these concepts will enable you to protect your communications and confidently navigate the digital domain.

S. Lekkala and P. Gurijala, *Security and Privacy for Modern Networks*, https://doi.org/10.1007/979-8-8688-0823-4_4

4.1 Leveraging Cryptography for Network Defense: Safeguarding Data in Transit

In the digital age, large amounts of sensitive data are transmitted via networks on a daily basis. Financial records, personal information, intellectual property, and secret corporate interactions are all transmitted throughout the digital landscape. Securing this data during transmission is critical, and cryptography plays an important part in this effort. This section delves into how cryptographic techniques are used to strengthen network defenses and secure the confidentiality, integrity, and validity of data in transit.

4.1.1 The Power of Cryptography: Safeguarding Data from Prying Eyes

Cryptography provides an effective mechanism for maintaining data confidentially by scrambling it with mathematical procedures. Encryption is the process of encrypting data so that it is unreadable to anyone who does not have the key. Even if attackers intercept encrypted data during transmission, they will be unable to decrypt its contents unless they have the right key.

Here's how encryption protects data confidentiality in network defense:

- **Securing Network Traffic:** Encrypting network traffic, such as that between web servers and user browsers (HTTPS), protects sensitive information like login credentials and financial data from eavesdropping.

- **Securing VPN Connections:** Virtual Private Networks (VPNs) encrypt data transmitted over public Wi-Fi networks, preventing spying or man-in-the-middle attacks.

- **Securing Email Communication:** Encrypting email communications protects important information against unauthorized access, even if attackers obtain access to email accounts.

4.1.2 Beyond Confidentiality: Ensuring Data Integrity and Authenticity

Cryptography protects more than simply confidentiality. It also plays an important function in maintaining data integrity and authenticity.

- **Data Integrity:** Hashing functions generate unique digital fingerprints (hashes) for data. Any changes to the data will result in a different hash value, making it easy to identify tampering during transmission.

- **Data Authenticity:** Digital signatures enable users to authenticate the authenticity and integrity of data. Users can electronically sign data using their private key, similar to how they would sign a physical document, and the recipient can validate the signature using the associated public key. This secures not just the sender's identity but also the data's integrity.

4.1.3 Cryptography: A Cornerstone of Network Security

Organizations can create secure communication channels by using strong cryptographic algorithms, which significantly reduces the risk of unauthorized data access, eavesdropping, and tampering when implemented and managed correctly. The parts that follow will go over advanced encryption algorithms and their different applications, as well as best practices for key management and how to employ cryptographic frameworks to establish a comprehensive and secure network.

4.2 Advanced Encryption Methods and Their Applications: A Deeper Dive into the Cryptographic Toolkit

Cryptography offers a diverse range of encryption techniques, each with its own set of advantages and applications. This section discusses different advanced encryption techniques that are crucial for protecting sensitive information in the digital age.

4.2.1 Beyond Symmetric Encryption: Exploring Asymmetric Cryptography

While symmetric encryption, which employs the same key for both encryption and decryption, is a straightforward solution, it does raise key management concerns. Asymmetric cryptography, also known as public-key cryptography, addresses this by using a key pair that consists of a public and a private key. The public key is made public, but the secret key remains hidden. Data encrypted with the public key can only be decrypted with the corresponding private key, making it a more secure and scalable solution for a variety of applications.

- **Digital Signatures:** Digital signatures, which are required for data integrity and authenticity, are based on asymmetric cryptography. Users sign data with their private key, and the recipient validates the signature with the corresponding public key to confirm the sender's legitimacy and data integrity.

- **Public Key Infrastructure (PKI):** PKI is a framework for managing digital certificates with public keys and associated identities. PKI enables secure communication and digital signatures by ensuring the authenticity and validity of public keys.

4.2.2 Exploring Advanced Encryption Algorithms

Modern encryption uses strong algorithms to jumble data safely. Here are some popular encryption algorithms and their applications:

- **Advanced Encryption Standard (AES):** A symmetric block cipher that has been adopted as the standard for encrypting sensitive information by the US federal government. AES is well-known for its efficiency and security, making it a popular choice for encrypting data both at rest on storage devices and in transit over networks.

- **Rivest–Shamir–Adleman (RSA):** A popular asymmetric algorithm for public-key cryptography. RSA is used for digital signatures, secure key exchange, and data encryption, particularly to protect online transactions and communication.

- **Elliptic Curve Cryptography (ECC):** A relatively recent technique that provides equal security to conventional algorithms such as RSA but with reduced key sizes. ECC's efficiency and small key sizes make it ideal for resource-constrained devices and applications that require high performance, such as mobile security and encrypted messaging.

4.2.3 Choosing the Right Encryption Method: A Balancing Act

The selection of a suitable encryption method is determined by various criteria, including

- **Security Requirements:** The degree of confidentiality, integrity, and validity necessary for the data.

- **Performance Considerations:** The computational power and processing speed made accessible for encryption and decoding.

- **Key Management Complexity:** The convenience of managing and securing cryptographic keys.

Understanding these advanced encryption algorithms and their applications allows you to make more educated decisions when adopting cryptographic solutions to protect sensitive information as part of your network security strategy. The following part will look at best practices for successful key management and implementing cryptographic frameworks to ensure that your cryptographic defenses remain effective.

4.3 Effective Key Management and Cryptographic Frameworks: The Pillars of Secure Encryption

The effectiveness of cryptography is dependent on the correct administration and security of cryptographic keys. Even the most strong encryption techniques become worthless if the keys are compromised. This section delves into best practices for effective key management and the use of cryptographic frameworks to develop a secure and well-coordinated approach to data encryption in your network security plan.

4.3.1 The Achilles' Heel of Encryption: The Importance of Key Management

Cryptographic keys are like the guardians of your encrypted data. Losing custody of a key can have severe repercussions, including unauthorized access to critical information. Here's why successful key management is critical:

- **Confidentiality Breach:** A leaked decryption key enables attackers to decrypt secret data, potentially revealing sensitive information.

- **Integrity Threats:** If an attacker acquires access to a signing key, they can fake digital signatures, impersonate authorized users, and tamper with data without detection.

- **Denial-of-Service Attacks:** Compromised keys must be revoked or disabled to prevent attackers from utilizing them to gain unwanted access or disrupt lawful decryption procedures.

4.3.2 Key Management Best Practices

Here are some important concepts for secure key management:

- **Strong Key Generation:** Strong random number generators are required to generate unpredictable and cryptographically safe keys.

- **Secure Key Storage:** To prevent unwanted access, keys should be securely held in hardware security modules (HSMs) or other tamper-proof locations.

- **Key Lifecycle Management:** Keys have a lifecycle, and adopting strong protocols for key creation, rotation, and destruction is critical to ensuring security.

- **Access Control:** Granting access to keys with least privilege and applying stringent access controls reduces the risk of unlawful key usage.

4.3.3 Cryptographic Frameworks: A Holistic Approach to Secure Communication

A cryptographic framework is a complete and standardized method for implementing cryptographic algorithms, key management methods, and digital signature protocols. Here's how frameworks help build a strong security posture:

- **Standardization:** Cryptographic frameworks ensure that encryption-enabled apps and systems behave consistently and interoperate seamlessly.

- **Security Best Practices:** Cryptographic frameworks ensure that encryption-enabled apps and systems behave consistently and interoperate seamlessly.

- **Simplified Integration:** Frameworks can help with the incorporation of cryptographic functions into applications, decreasing development time and potential errors.

4.3.4 Popular Cryptographic Frameworks

There are several well-established cryptographic frameworks available, each with unique strengths and applications. Here are some instances:

- **OpenSSL:** A popular open source toolkit that provides a number of cryptographic functions, algorithms, and protocols.

- **Microsoft CryptoAPI (CAPI):** A Windows-specific framework that provides cryptography services to apps operating on Windows platforms.

- **Java Cryptography Architecture (JCA):** A framework integrated into the Java platform that allows developers to incorporate cryptographic features into Java applications.

By employing effective key management methods and leveraging existing cryptographic frameworks, you may maintain the efficacy of your cryptographic defenses while also protecting the confidentiality, integrity, and authenticity of your sensitive data. This finishes Chapter 4, which provides you with a thorough understanding of cryptography and its applications in network security. The chapters that follow will look at various security architectures, protocols, and best practices for building a strong and layered approach to network security.

CHAPTER 5

Ensuring Robust Authentication and Access Management

Controlling access to network resources is a critical component of any effective security plan. This chapter delves into the key ideas of authentication and access management. We will look at modern authentication approaches and technology that validate user identities. We'll look into approaches for fine-grained authorization, which ensures users only have access to the resources they require. Finally, we'll look at ways for streamlining identity management and access control models in order to simplify administration and improve security. Understanding and adopting these concepts allows you to build a strong system that protects your network resources while reducing the danger of unauthorized access.

5.1 Modern Authentication Techniques and Technologies: Beyond Passwords

In today's digital landscape, typical username and password combinations are no longer enough to ensure safe authentication. Cybercriminals have advanced tools to crack passwords, and static credentials provide

S. Lekkala and P. Gurijala, *Security and Privacy for Modern Networks*, https://doi.org/10.1007/979-8-8688-0823-4_5

a single point of failure if compromised. This section delves into current authentication approaches and technologies, which provide a more comprehensive and tiered approach to user verification.

5.1.1 Moving Beyond Passwords: Multifactor Authentication (MFA)

Multifactor authentication (MFA) provides an additional degree of protection to the login process. In addition to a username and password, MFA requires users to supply at least one extra factor for authentication. This additional component may be

- **Something You Know:** A passphrase, security question, or secret PIN.

- **Something You Have:** A physical token, phone app generating one-time codes, or a security key.

- **Something You Are:** Biometric authentication using fingerprints impressions, facial recognition, or iris scans.

MFA dramatically minimizes the danger of unauthorized access, even if attackers are able to acquire a user's password. Without the additional element, they will be unable to obtain access to the protected resource.

5.1.2 Beyond Static Credentials: Embracing Adaptive Authentication

Static passwords are insecure and susceptible to brute-force attacks. Adaptive authentication uses a more dynamic approach, accounting for a variety of factors during the login process. Here is how adaptive authentication improves security:

- **Risk-Based Authentication:** The system analyzes login attempts by location, device type, and time of day. Suspicious activity, such as login attempts from unfamiliar locations or devices, requires additional authentication measures, such as MFA, for login attempts from odd locations or times.

- **Continuous Monitoring:** User behavior and activity patterns are being observed. Unusual login patterns, such as a rapid surge from a new location, may require further authentication or temporarily lock the account.

5.1.3 Emerging Technologies: Biometrics and Passwordless Authentication

Biometric authentication uses unique physical or behavioral traits, such as fingerprints, facial recognition, or voice patterns, to verify user identities. Passwordless authentication completely eliminates the need for static passwords, relying instead on elements such as secure tokens or biometric verification for login.

5.1.4 Choosing the Right Authentication Method: A Balancing Act

The selection of an acceptable authentication mechanism is dependent on numerous criteria, including

- **Security Requirements:** The level of security needed to protect the resources being accessed.

- **User Convenience:** Balancing security with a user-friendly experience is vital for user adoption.

- **Scalability and Cost:** The feasibility of implementing and managing the chosen authentication technique for your organization.

Understanding these modern authentication approaches and technologies enables you to adopt a layered approach to user verification that improves security, minimizes the danger of illegal access, and provides a more convenient user experience. The following sections will look at fine-grained authorization and policy enforcement strategies for improving your access control processes.

5.2 Fine-Grained Authorization and Policy Enforcement: Granular Control over Access

5.2.1 Beyond All-or-Nothing Access: The Need for Granular Control

Traditional access control models frequently provide users access to whole systems or resources. This all-or-nothing strategy can be unduly permissive, giving users access to data or features they don't absolutely need. Fine-grained authorization takes a more nuanced approach, providing more specific control over user permissions.

5.2.2 The Power of Granularity: Defining Access Levels and Permissions

Fine-grained authorization allows you to set several access levels with precise rights for each level. This is how it works:

- **Users and Roles:** Users are allocated roles, and each position has a defined set of permissions.

- **Permissions:** Permissions specify the activities a user can take on a resource, such as reading, writing, editing, or deleting it.

- **Resource-Specific Controls:** Granular control can be applied to individual resources or data sets inside a larger system.

5.2.3 Policy Enforcement: Putting Granularity into Action

Access control policies specify the rules that regulate user access to resources. These policies are implemented by authorization servers or access control lists (ACLs), which look at user credentials, assigned roles, and associated permissions to determine whether access should be given or refused.

5.2.4 Benefits of Fine-Grained Authorization

Implementing fine-grained authorization offers several advantages:

- **Reduced Risk**: By limiting user access to only the resources and capabilities they need, you may reduce the potential damage caused by hacked accounts.

- **Enhanced Compliance**: Granular control makes it easier to comply with industry rules and data protection obligations.

- **Improved Security Posture**: A multilayered approach to access control improves your overall security posture.

51

5.2.5 Implementing Fine-Grained Authorization

Here are some important concerns for developing fine-grained authorization:

- Role-Based Access Control (RBAC) is a frequently used mechanism for assigning permissions based on user role.

- Attribute-Based Access Control (ABAC) uses a dynamic approach to decision-making by considering various factors, such as user location, device type, and data sensitivity.

- Identity and Access Management (IAM) solutions centralize user management, authentication, and authorization, making it easier to develop and enforce access control policies.

By implementing fine-grained authorization and access control policies, you can create a more secure and controlled environment within your network, ensuring that users only have access to the resources they require to complete their activities successfully. The following part will look at techniques for streamlining identity management and access control models in order to improve security and administrative efficiency.

5.3 Streamlining Identity Management and Access Control Models

Simplifying identity and access management is critical to ensuring a secure and efficient network. This section investigates methods for simplifying these processes.

5.3.1 Challenges of Identity Management

Managing user identities and access rights across a big network can be a difficult undertaking. Here are a few prevalent challenges:

- **User Provisioning and Deprovisioning**: It is critical to effectively add new users, assign roles, and revoke access when users leave the business.

- **Directory Synchronization**: Keeping user identities and access controls consistent across systems can be time-consuming and error-prone.

- **Access Reviews and Audits**: Regularly assessing user access and performing security audits are critical for maintaining a secure posture.

5.3.2 Streamlining Identity Management

Here are some strategies for streamlining identity management:

- **Identity and Access Management (IAM) Systems:** As previously stated, IAM systems centralize user management, authentication, and authorization, which simplifies administration.

- **Automated User Provisioning and Deprovisioning:** Automating these operations decreases manual labor and lowers the chance of human error.

- **Self-Service Password Management:** Allowing users to reset their passwords or update their profiles alleviates administrative burden.

5.3.3 Simplifying Access Control Models

Here are some methods for streamlining access control models:

- **Standardization:** The use of uniform role-based access control (RBAC) models across several systems minimizes complexity.

- **Least Privilege:** Allowing users only the minimum amount of access necessary for their jobs reduces the potential damage caused by hacked accounts.

- **Regular Reviews and Audits:** Regularly evaluating user access and conducting security audits ensures that access controls are still effective.

5.3.4 Optimizing Identity Management and Access Control

Implementing these solutions will help you streamline identity management, simplify access control models, and decrease administrative overhead. This not only increases security, but also the user experience and operational efficiency. This finishes Chapter 5, which has provided you with the expertise to construct powerful authentication and access control systems.

CHAPTER 6

Fortifying Wired Network Infrastructures

The physical infrastructure must be secure before any robust network security posture can be established. This chapter delves further into the specific concerns for protecting wired network setups. We will look at ways for protecting high-speed and fiber-optic network systems, which are becoming more common in today's data-driven environment. We will address both physical and logical risks to wired network integrity and availability. Finally, we'll look at best practices for hardening wired network infrastructure, such as device setup, access control, and vulnerability management, to help create a more resilient and secure network environment. Understanding and applying these procedures will dramatically reduce the risk of unauthorized access, data breaches, and disruptions to key network operations.

S. Lekkala and P. Gurijala, *Security and Privacy for Modern Networks*, https://doi.org/10.1007/979-8-8688-0823-4_6

6.1 Securing High-Speed and Fiber Optic Network Systems

High-speed and fiber-optic networks are the foundation of modern data communication, providing superior speed, reliability, and bandwidth when compared to traditional copper cabling. However, securing these complex network systems necessitates specific measures to mitigate potential vulnerabilities.

6.1.1 Understanding the Advantages and Security Implications of High-Speed Networks

- **Increased Transmission Speeds:** High-speed networks, such as Gigabit Ethernet and 10 Gigabit Ethernet, facilitate quick data transfer, making them ideal for big data centers and cloud computing settings. However, their fast speeds make them ideal targets for attackers looking to intercept sensitive data in transit.

- **Fiber-Optic Security Advantages:** Fiber-optic lines transport data using light pulses, which are intrinsically more difficult to intercept than electrical signals in copper cables. However, physical security of fiber-optic cables is still critical, as damage or manipulation can impede network connectivity.

6.1.2 Securing Fiber-Optic Networks

- **Physical Security:** Implementing physical safety for fiber-optic connections is critical. This includes securing cable entry sites, using conduit for subterranean wiring, and installing intrusion detection systems to detect unlawful access attempts.

- **Encryption:** Encrypting data sent over high-speed networks adds an extra degree of protection, rendering it unreadable even if intercepted.

6.1.3 Hardening Network Devices for High-Speed Environments

- **Secure Configuration:** In high-speed environments, network devices such as switches and routers should be configured with strong passwords, unneeded ports disabled, and firmware updated on a regular basis to mitigate potential vulnerabilities.

- **Network Segmentation:** Divide the network into smaller segments using firewalls to limit the possible damage caused by a security breach while also improving overall network security.

6.1.4 Security Considerations for Wireless Network Integration

While this chapter focuses on wired networks, securing the convergence points where wired and wireless networks meet is critical. Implementing access control techniques and configuring VLANs correctly can help prevent illegal access from wireless devices seeking to infiltrate the wired network.

Understanding the particular characteristics of high-speed and fiber-optic networks, as well as applying these security measures, can protect the integrity, confidentiality, and availability of data passing via your wired network infrastructure. The parts that follow will look at a broader spectrum of dangers to wired networks, as well as effective practices for mitigating them.

6.2 Addressing Physical and Logical Threats to Wired Networks

Securing wired networks necessitates a comprehensive strategy that tackles both physical and logical weaknesses. This section delves into the various sorts of threats that might jeopardize the integrity and availability of your network, as well as mitigation measures for each.

6.2.1 Physical Security Threats

Physical security is frequently the first line of defense for wired networks. Here are some frequent physical risks you should be aware of:

- **Unauthorized Access:** Physical access to network devices, cabling, or server rooms enables attackers to tamper with equipment, steal data, or disrupt network operations. Implementing access control mechanisms such as security cameras, badge readers, and restricted access protocols is critical.

- **Environmental Threats:** Environmental elements such as fire, power outages, and severe temperatures can all harm network equipment and impair communication. It is critical to put in place appropriate environmental controls, backup power supply, and disaster recovery strategies.

- **Equipment Tampering:** Malicious actors may exploit network equipment to install malware, steal data, or disrupt network traffic. Regularly examining equipment, implementing access control, and following stringent physical security protocols can help to reduce this danger.

6.2.2 Logical Security Threats

Logical security risks attack the software and protocols that run on your wired network. Here are some common logical threats to consider:

- **Malware and Viruses:** Malicious software can infect network equipment, compromising data integrity and confidentiality. Implementing strong antivirus and anti-malware solutions with regular updates is critical.

- **Network Attacks:** Attackers can use weaknesses in network protocols or devices to obtain unwanted access, steal data, or disrupt network operations. Updating network devices and software with security fixes is critical.

- **Man-in-the-Middle Attacks:** These attacks include intercepting communication between two network devices, perhaps eavesdropping on data or modifying traffic. Strong encryption and network segmentation help reduce this risk.

- **Denial-of-Service (DoS) Attacks:** These attacks flood network resources with traffic, preventing genuine users from accessing them. Implementing intrusion detection and prevention systems (IDS/IPS) and providing appropriate bandwidth capacity can aid in the defense against DoS attacks.

6.2.3 Securing Network Protocols

Network protocols such as TCP/IP are susceptible to exploitation. Implementing security measures such as firewalls, intrusion detection systems, and secure network topologies can help to reduce these risks.

6.2.4 Building a Defense-in-Depth Strategy

A tiered approach to security, often known as defense-in-depth, is required to properly address both physical and logical threats. This entails deploying several security measures at various locations throughout the network architecture to establish redundancy and reduce the possible impact of a successful attack.

Understanding these dangers and applying the necessary protections will dramatically improve the security posture of your wired network architecture. The following part will go over best practices for hardening wired networks and maintaining a secure environment.

6.3 Adopting Best Practices for Wired Network Hardening

Securing your wired network infrastructure entails more than merely installing network devices and connecting them with wires. A proactive approach to network hardening is required to reduce vulnerabilities and establish a stronger security posture. This section delves into the best practices for hardening wired networks, allowing you to protect your essential network assets.

6.3.1 Hardening Network Devices

- **Secure Configuration:** To address potential vulnerabilities, network components such as switches, routers, and firewalls should be rigorously setup, with strong passwords, unneeded ports shut, and automatic upgrades enabled. Use the manufacturer's recommended best practices for secure configuration specific to each device model.

- **Firmware Updates:** Update network device firmware on a regular basis to patch vulnerabilities and guarantee they are operating with the most up-to-date security features. Schedule automated updates wherever possible to reduce the window of vulnerability.

- **Access Control:** Implement granular access restrictions on network devices, limiting access to authorized workers and valid purposes. Use role-based access control (RBAC) to provide permissions depending on individual user requirements.

6.3.2 Network Segmentation

Divide your network into smaller regions using firewalls to improve security. Here's how segmentation improves your network:

- **Reduced Attack Surface:** Segmenting your network reduces the possible effect of a security compromise. If one segment is compromised, the attacker's access is limited to that segment only, reducing the spread of the attack to other vital resources.

- **Improved Traffic Flow:** Segmenting the network according to traffic types can improve network performance by separating high-bandwidth traffic from sensitive data flows.

6.3.3 Implementing Network Security Controls

- **Firewalls:** Firewalls serve as the first line of protection, filtering incoming and outgoing network traffic using specified security policies. Configure firewalls to allow only authorized traffic while blocking suspicious or malicious traffic attempting to enter your network.

- **Intrusion Detection and Prevention Systems (IDS/IPS):** These systems monitor network traffic for unusual behavior and can detect or actively prevent potential security breaches. IDS/IPS systems can be extremely useful in identifying and mitigating various network attacks.

6.3.4 Vulnerability Management

- **Vulnerability Scanning:** Scan your network's devices and infrastructure for vulnerabilities on a regular basis. These scans can detect potential vulnerabilities that attackers may exploit. Prioritize repairing significant vulnerabilities found during scans to reduce the window of exposure.

- **Patch Management:** Create a thorough patch management strategy to ensure the timely deployment of security patches for network devices, operating systems, and applications. Automate patch deployment whenever possible to speed up the process and reduce the risk of unpatched vulnerabilities.

6.3.5 Maintaining Secure Network Documentation

Maintaining correct and up-to-date network documentation is critical for successful network security management. The documentation should include

- **Network Diagrams:** Visual representations of network topology, which includes devices, connections, and segmentation.

- **Security Policies:** These include security baselines, access control rules, and firewall configurations.

- **Asset Inventory:** A thorough list of all network devices, software applications, and security settings.

By adhering to these best practices for wired network hardening, you may greatly improve the security posture of your network infrastructure. This finishes Chapter 6, which provides you with the knowledge and methods necessary to protect your wired network environment. The chapters that follow will go over wireless network security, network security monitoring, and incident response best practices in order to construct a comprehensive network security strategy.

CHAPTER 7

Wireless Network Protection Strategies

In today's mobile environment, wireless networks have become an essential component of our daily lives. However, the inherent openness and flexibility of wireless communication present distinct security challenges. In this chapter, we look at effective wireless network security solutions. We'll look at ways to improve security in wireless protocols and infrastructures; protect growing cellular networks like 4G, 5G, and beyond; and investigate next-generation Wi-Fi security techniques. Understanding these tactics and adopting the necessary protections will help mitigate your wireless networks from risks caused by unauthorized access and potential dangers.

7.1 Enhancing Security in Wireless Protocols and Infrastructures

Wireless networks' open nature creates distinct security issues as compared to conventional connections. This section delves into strategies for increasing security in wireless protocols and infrastructure components to protect your wireless connection.

S. Lekkala and P. Gurijala, *Security and Privacy for Modern Networks*, https://doi.org/10.1007/979-8-8688-0823-4_7

7.1.1 Securing Wireless Protocols: The Backbone of Secure Communication

Wireless protocols specify the communication language used by devices on a wireless network. Here's how we can improve security at the fundamental level:

- **Encryption: The Shield Against Eavesdropping**

  - Implementing strong encryption techniques such as WPA3 (Wi-Fi Protected Access 3) is critical. WPA3 improves on previous versions, making it substantially more resistant to decryption efforts by unauthorized users. Encryption scrambles data communications, making them illegible to anybody without the decryption key.

- **Authentication: Verification for Access Control**

  - Enforce strong authentication measures, such as 802.1x, to ensure that only authorized devices can join to your Wi-Fi network. 802.1x uses a centralized authentication server to validate user and device credentials before providing network access. This two-factor authentication method stops unwanted devices from posing as genuine ones and gaining access to your network.

7.1.2 Hardening Wireless Network Infrastructure: Securing the Gateways

Wireless access points (WAPs) serve as gateways between devices and wireless networks. Here's how to improve their security posture:

- **Secure Configuration: The Foundation of a Strong Defense**

  - WAPs must be carefully configured. This includes creating secure and unique passwords for administrative access, turning off unnecessary features to reduce potential vulnerabilities, and allowing automated firmware updates to guarantee you have the most recent security fixes installed.

- **Access Control: Granular Permissions for Enhanced Security**

  - Implement granular access control techniques for your wireless network. Using MAC address filtering, you can restrict access to just approved devices. MAC addresses are unique identifiers allocated to network devices, and filtering enables you to choose which devices can connect to your network.

- **Guest Network: Segregation for Increased Protection**

  - Consider setting up a separate guest network for visitors and devices that do not need access to your internal network services. This division helps to separate guest traffic and reduces potential security threats if a guest device is exploited. Keep guest traffic segregated to prevent it from spreading laterally and endangering crucial data on your internal network.

7.1.3 Network Segmentation: Compartmentalizing Your Network for Enhanced Defense

As described in Chapter 6, network segmentation is equally applicable to wireless networks. Divide your wireless network into discrete areas, such as for employees, guests, and Internet of Things (IoT) devices, to improve security. Here's how segmentation can improve your wireless network:

- **Reduced Attack Surface:** Segmenting your network reduces the possible effect of a security compromise. If a device on one segment is compromised, the attacker's access is limited to that segment only, reducing the spread of the attacks to other key resources on different segments.

- **Improved Security Posture:** Segmentation enables you to apply more granular security rules to each segment based on the type of traffic and devices that access it. This layered strategy improves the overall security posture of your wireless network.

Segmentation enables you to apply more granular security rules to each segment based on the type of traffic and devices that access it. This layered strategy improves the overall security posture of your wireless network.

7.2 Safeguarding Evolving Cellular Networks (4G, 5G, and Beyond)

The cellular network landscape is rapidly changing, with 4G (LTE) and 5G technologies providing considerable improvements in speed, capacity, and latency compared to prior generations. However, these improvements bring with them new security concerns, necessitating the adaptation of our defensive measures. This section investigates solutions for protecting cellular networks as they develop.

7.2.1 Securing 4G and 5G Networks: A Multilayered Approach

Securing 4G and 5G networks requires a comprehensive approach that includes a variety of security techniques.

- **Encryption: The Bedrock of Data Confidentiality**

    - Modern cellular networks use strong encryption algorithms like AES (Advanced Encryption Standard) to scramble data flows between mobile devices and cell towers. This encryption ensures the confidentiality of your data, rendering it unreadable even if intercepted by intruders. However, for maximum security, verify that your mobile device is configured to use these encryption protocols.

- **Network Infrastructure Security: Protecting the Core**

    - Modern cellular networks use strong encryption algorithms like AES (Advanced Encryption Standard) to scramble data flows between mobile devices and cell towers. This encryption ensures the confidentiality of your data, rendering it unreadable even if intercepted by intruders. However, for maximum security, verify that your mobile device is configured to use these encryption protocols.

- **Device Security: Your Line of Defense**

    - Your mobile device's security posture has a substantial impact on the overall security of the cellular network. Here's how you can improve your device's security:

- **Keeping Your Device Updated:** Regularly update your device's operating system and applications with the most recent security updates. These updates frequently address vulnerabilities that could be exploited by hackers.

- **Strong Passwords or Biometric Authentication:** Use strong passwords or activate biometric authentication (fingerprint scan, face recognition) for device access. This provides an additional degree of security to prevent unwanted parties from gaining access to your device and potentially jeopardizing your cellular network connection.

7.2.2 Securing Mobile Device Communication: Extending Your Safeguards

While network providers and device security are critical, here are some extra precautions you may take to protect your mobile device communication:

- **VPNs for Enhanced Protection:** When using public Wi-Fi networks, consider using a Virtual Private Network (VPN). A VPN encrypts all of your device's Internet traffic, providing an additional layer of security and making it more difficult for attackers to intercept your data over insecure Wi-Fi networks.

- **Phishing and Malware Awareness: The Human Firewall**

  - Mobile devices are vulnerable to phishing attacks and malware outbreaks. Teach yourself and others how to recognize and avoid questionable texts, emails, and downloads. Phishing attempts frequently attempt to deceive you into clicking on malicious links or opening attachments, which can infect your device and potentially disclose your cellular network connection. Being aware of these hazards and practicing caution can considerably lower your chances of falling victim to such attacks.

Understanding these security issues and putting them into action will help you and others create a more secure cellular network environment. The following part will look at next-generation Wi-Fi security techniques that are being researched to improve wireless network defense.

7.3 Next-Generation Wi-Fi Security Techniques

The world of Wi-Fi security is continuously changing, with new solutions developing to combat the ever-changing threat landscape. As attackers develop increasingly advanced ways, the necessity for strong Wi-Fi security grows more crucial. This section looks at several promising advances in Wi-Fi security that are expected to play an important role in protecting our wireless connections in the future.

7.3.1 WPA3 Enhancements: Building Upon a Strong Foundation

WPA3 (Wi-Fi Protected Access 3) was introduced as a significant improvement over its predecessor, WPA2. Here's how WPA3 strengthens Wi-Fi security:

- **More Robust Encryption:** WPA3 uses stronger encryption techniques, making it far more difficult for attackers to break the encryption and access your data. These developments increase its resistance against brute-force attacks and other decoding attempts.

- **Improved Password Hashing:** WPA3 uses stronger password hashing algorithms, making it more difficult for attackers to acquire credentials, even if they intercept them in a network breach. Password hashing uses one-way cryptographic techniques to convert passwords into a safe string of characters, rendering them unreadable in their original form.

- **Enhanced Protection Against Offline Dictionary Attacks:** WPA3-SAE (Simultaneous Authentication of Equals) is a variation of WPA3 that provides enhanced security against offline dictionary attacks. Offline dictionary attacks try a huge number of pre-computed password combinations to crack a password. WPA3-SAE complicates this process by introducing an additional layer of defense.

7.3.2 Simplified Security for Limited User Interfaces: WPA3-OWE

WPA3-OWE (Opportunistic Wireless Encryption) addresses a unique issue in the expanding world of Internet-connected devices. Many devices, especially those with limited user interfaces, such as smart home appliances, might be difficult to configure using complex passwords. WPA3-OWE provides a simpler method to security for these devices while yet providing strong protection. Here's how WPA3-OWE strikes this balance:

- **Simplified Key Derivation:** WPA3-OWE simplifies the key derivation process, reducing the need to manually configure complex passwords for devices with limited user interfaces. This allows you to safely connect these devices to your Wi-Fi network.

- **Strong Security Despite Simplification:** Despite its reduced approach, WPA3-OWE provides a high level of security. It uses powerful cryptographic algorithms to ensure that only authorized devices can connect to your network.

7.3.3 The Future of Wi-Fi Security: Continuous Innovation

The creation of new security techniques is a continuous process. As Wi-Fi technology advances, we should expect to see new security methods and processes. Here are some promising places to explore:

- **Post-Quantum Cryptography:** As quantum computing technology advances, it may represent a danger to current encryption techniques. Post-Quantum Cryptography focuses on creating new encryption algorithms that can withstand potential quantum computer attacks.

- **Zero-Trust Security:** Zero-trust security principles can be applied to Wi-Fi networks to improve security. This method believes that no device or user is inherently trustworthy and requires ongoing verification before allowing access to network resources.

- **Artificial Intelligence (AI) for Threat Detection:**
  Artificial intelligence-powered systems can be used to
  analyze network traffic and detect potential security
  problems in real time. This can assist detect and
  prevent security vulnerabilities before they cause
  substantial damage.

We can make our wireless connections more secure by applying
these next-generation Wi-Fi security strategies and remaining up to date
on emerging improvements. The following chapter will look at network
security monitoring procedures and incident response strategies for
proactively identifying and mitigating potential security risks.

CHAPTER 8

Designing Secure Network Architectures

Building a safe network environment entails more than merely installing network devices and connecting them with wires. A well-designed network architecture is the foundation for a strong security posture. This chapter discusses the principles and practices of developing secure network architectures. We'll look at ways for developing robust and secure network designs, implementing a thorough defense-in-depth strategy, using network segmentation to promote isolation, and adhering to secure network design principles. Understanding and utilizing these concepts will dramatically improve the security of your network architecture.

8.1 Crafting Resilient and Secure Network Designs

The design phase of your network architecture is critical for building a solid security foundation. A secure network architecture, like a sturdy foundation for a house, supports your network's overall security posture. Here are some important factors for designing resilient and secure networks.

8.1.1 Identifying Security Requirements

Before getting into the technical parts of design, it is critical to understand your individual security requirements. This includes performing a security risk assessment to determine the sorts of data you handle, any regulatory compliance requirements you must meet, and your organization's overall risk tolerance. Here are some of the common regulatory compliance requirements that organizations may need to consider – PCI, DSS, HIPAA, or GDPR. Understanding these elements enables you to customize your network security design in order to successfully minimize potential threats.

8.1.2 Threat Modeling

Proactively identifying potential threats and weaknesses is a vital step in developing a safe network. Threat modeling is brainstorming and documenting potential attack vectors that your network may encounter. By taking these dangers into account during the design phase, you can put in place safeguards and design aspects that make it more difficult for attackers to exploit network vulnerabilities.

8.1.3 Least Privilege Access Control

The idea of least privilege states that users and devices should only be given the minimum amount of access necessary to complete their responsibilities. This reduces the possible damage if a security compromise happens. For example, a typical user account should not have administrator access to important systems. By using least privilege, you may reduce the attack surface and potential damage of compromised accounts.

8.1.4 Redundancy and Failover Mechanisms

Building resiliency into your network design is critical to assuring continuous operation during outages or equipment failures. This may include deploying redundant network paths, power supplies, crucial network devices, and usage of high availability clustering. Redundancy ensures that if one path or device fails, another can take over and keep the network functioning. This not only increases uptime, but also reduces disruption to vital business activities that rely on the network.

By including these factors during the design phase, you can build the groundwork for a durable and secure network architecture. The following section delves into a key security concept: defense-in-depth.

8.2 Deploying a Comprehensive Defense-in-Depth Approach

A layered security technique, often known as defense-in-depth, is required for effective network security. This technique entails establishing different security measures throughout the network infrastructure. Here's what makes defense-in-depth so effective:

- **Multilayered Protection:** By using a layered approach, even if an attacker manages to get beyond one security restriction, they will still face additional obstacles before reaching important network resources. Imagine a castle with various walls and defenses. An attacker would have to break through each layer to get access to the center stronghold.

- **Enhanced Security Posture:** Defense-in-depth improves overall network security by reducing the possible impact of a successful attack. Even if one layer is compromised, the others can help to contain the attack and keep attackers from accessing sensitive data or interrupting essential systems.

- **Improved Threat Detection:** The numerous security measures placed across the network can serve as early warning systems. Monitoring activity at various points within the network can help you detect and prevent attacks before they do substantial damage.

Examples of Defense-in-Depth Controls

- **Perimeter Security (Firewalls):** Firewalls are the first line of protection, screening incoming and outgoing traffic according to security regulations.

- **Network Segmentation:** By dividing your network into smaller regions, you can minimize the propagation of a security compromise.

- **Intrusion Detection and Prevention Systems (IDS/IPS):** These systems scan network traffic for unusual activity and can detect or actively prevent potential security breaches.

- **Endpoint Security:** Protecting individual endpoints such as laptops, desktops, and servers is critical to overall network security. This can include installing antivirus software, enforcing strong password policies, and updating devices with security patches.

You can dramatically improve your network's overall security posture by adhering to the defense-in-depth concepts and layering security controls. The next sections will go over network segmentation and general secure network design principles to help you increase your network's defense mechanisms.

8.3 Deploying a Comprehensive Defense-in-Depth Approach

A layered security technique, often known as defense-in-depth, is required for effective network security. This technique entails deploying several security controls at various locations along the network architecture, resulting in a layered security paradigm. Consider a medieval fortress with several rings of walls and defenses. To get to the center, an attacker would have to break through each layer. Similarly, defense-in-depth raises many barriers for attackers, making it much more difficult to infiltrate your network and access important resources.

Here's why defense-in-depth is so effective.

8.3.1 Multilayered Protection

Even if an attacker gets past one security measure, they will face additional obstacles before reaching important network resources. Each layer serves as a separate line of protection, creating redundancy and making it more difficult for attackers to succeed.

8.3.2 Enhanced Security Posture

Defense-in-depth improves your entire network security posture. If one layer is compromised, the others can help to confine the attack and keep attackers from compromising sensitive data or interrupting vital systems. It promotes a more secure environment.

8.3.3 Improved Threat Detection

The numerous security measures placed across the network serve as early warning systems. Monitoring activity at various points within the network can help you detect and prevent attacks before they do substantial damage. These security measures might raise red flags and warn you to any questionable activity.

Examples of Defense-in-Depth Controls

- **Perimeter Security (Firewalls):** Firewalls serve as the first line of defense, screening incoming and outgoing traffic using specified security policies. They monitor and control network traffic, enabling only approved communications to pass through.

- **Network Segmentation:** Divide your network into smaller segments to restrict the spread of a security compromise. By segmenting the network depending on function (e.g., administration, user traffic, guest network), security sensitivity, or device type, you can confine an attack to a specific segment and prevent it from spreading throughout the network.

- **Intrusion Detection and Prevention Systems (IDS/IPS):** These systems constantly scan network traffic for unusual activity. IDS systems can identify risks, whereas IPS systems can actively prevent them by blocking malicious traffic or implementing other countermeasures.

- **Endpoint Security:** Individual devices such as laptops, desktops, and servers must be secure in order for the network to function properly. This includes deploying antivirus and anti-malware software, enforcing strong password policies and multifactor authentication, and updating devices with security patches to address vulnerabilities.

Implementing a defense-in-depth approach and layering security policies can greatly improve your network's overall security posture. The next sections will go over network segmentation and general secure network design principles to help you increase your network's defenses.

8.4 Utilizing Network Segmentation for Improved Isolation

Network segmentation is an effective strategy for improving network security. It entails separating your network into smaller, isolated portions based on predetermined parameters. Consider a large room separated into distinct sections with limited access between them. Network segmentation implements a similar principle within your network, isolating various components to increase security and network efficiency.

Here's how network segmentation works.

8.4.1 Dividing the Network

You can segment your network based on various factors, such as

- **Function:** Separating traffic kinds such as administrative, user, and guest traffic into distinct segments can improve network security and performance. For example, segmenting administrative traffic onto a separate network can assist prevent it from interfering with regular user traffic while also potentially improving overall network efficiency.

- **Security Sensitivity:** Segmenting networks based on data sensitivity enables more strict security measures for essential resources. For example, you may put financial data or customer information in a distinct segment with greater access controls and monitoring than a segment with less critical data.

- **Device Type:** Networks can be segmented by device type (e.g., servers, desktops, and IoT devices) to help contain threats and prevent them from propagating throughout the network. Isolating IoT devices on a separate segment reduces the potential damage if one is compromised. This compartmentalization ensures that a security breach on one segment does not result in automatic access to other vital network resources.

8.4.2 Benefits of Network Segmentation

Network segmentation offers several advantages for network security:

- **Reduced Attack Surface:** Segmenting your network reduces the possible effect of a security compromise. If an attacker gains access to a single segment, their ability to move laterally and access other vital network resources is limited. This compartmentalization serves to contain the attack and reduce the possible damage.

- **Improved Security Enforcement:** Segmentation enables you to apply more granular security measures to each segment. You can adapt the security measures to meet the specific requirements of the devices and data in that segment. For example, you could impose stronger security regulations and implement additional security controls on the section that contains sensitive financial data.

- **Enhanced Network Performance:** Segmenting traffic can improve network performance by minimizing congestion in specific network segments. Separating different types of traffic allows you to manage bandwidth more efficiently and avoid bottlenecks, which could slow down vital network processes. Separating user traffic from high-bandwidth activities like video conferencing can help ensure that everyone has a better user experience by reducing congestion and latency, and also promotes better resource allocation.

Overall, network segmentation is an effective security method that can improve your network's overall security posture. Isolating various sections of your network allows you to limit the harm caused by security breaches, improve the effectiveness of your security measures, and increase the overall efficiency of your network operations.

8.5 Secure Network Design Principles

Now that we've covered fundamental concepts like defense-in-depth and network segmentation, let's look at some general secure network design principles to consider while developing your network architecture. Here are some basic principles to follow.

8.5.1 Maintain a Minimal Attack Surface

The notion of limiting the attack surface is critical to network security. This includes limiting the amount of potential entry points that attackers can use to gain access to your network. Here's how to do this:

- **Minimize Exposed Services:** Only deploy network services that are strictly required for business operations. Turn off unnecessary services and functionalities on network devices to reduce the attack surface and potential vulnerabilities.

- **Harden Network Devices**: Update network devices (firewalls, routers, and switches) with the most recent security patches and firmware updates. This addresses known vulnerabilities that attackers may attempt to exploit.

- **Implement Strong Authentication:** Enforce strong authentication protocols on all network access points, including user accounts, administrative access, and remote connections. This increases the difficulty for unauthorized users to gain access to your network.

8.5.2 Implement the Principle of Least Privilege

As previously discussed, the principle of least privilege states that users and devices should only be granted the minimum level of access necessary to complete their tasks. This principle applies to network devices and services, as well as user accounts. Excessive permissions can result in vulnerabilities if an account or device is compromised.

8.5.3 Prioritize Secure Network Segmentation

Network segmentation, as discussed in the previous section, is an important security principle. Isolating different parts of your network allows you to limit the potential damage from a security breach while also improving overall network security.

8.5.4 Maintain Network Visibility and Monitoring

Maintaining high network visibility is critical for detecting and responding to security threats quickly. Use network monitoring tools to detect suspicious activity, possible intrusions, and anomalies in your network traffic. This enables you to take proactive steps to mitigate threats before they cause significant damage.

8.5.5 Implement a Defense-in-Depth Approach

A layered security approach, as previously discussed, is required for strong network security. By implementing various security controls throughout your network infrastructure, you create multiple barriers for attackers to overcome. This significantly reduces their ability to infiltrate your network and gain access to critical resources.

8.5.6 Document Your Network Design

Maintaining and managing security requires well-documented network architecture and security policies. Clear documentation enables your IT team to understand the network layout, security controls, and access control policies. This enables more efficient troubleshooting, security audits, and future network modifications.

By following these secure network design principles, you can create a network architecture that is both functional and includes strong security measures to protect your valuable data and resources from potential threats.

CHAPTER 9

Data Security in the Age of Connectivity

This chapter delves into the critical topic of data security in today's interconnected world. As organizations collect, store, and transmit massive amounts of data, maintaining its confidentiality, integrity, and privacy becomes critical. This chapter looks at a three-pronged approach to data security in the digital age. First, we'll explore the ever-changing legal landscape of data privacy (Section 9.1). Understanding data privacy laws and compliance obligations is critical for navigating the regulatory landscape and protecting your organization from potential legal consequences. Next, we'll look at innovative data protection and encryption strategies (Section 9.2) that can protect sensitive information throughout its lifecycle. Finally, we'll look at how to ensure data integrity and confidentiality (Section 9.3). This section will go over steps to ensure that your data remains unaltered and that unauthorized access is prevented, thereby protecting the trustworthiness and privacy of your valuable information. Understanding and implementing these data security practices allows you to effectively mitigate risks and build trust with your stakeholders in the digital age.

© The Editor(s) (if applicable) and The Author(s), under exclusive license to APress Media, LLC, part of Springer Nature 2024
S. Lekkala and P. Gurijala, *Security and Privacy for Modern Networks*,
https://doi.org/10.1007/979-8-8688-0823-4_9

9.1 Navigating Data Privacy Laws and Compliance Obligations

In the age of big data and ubiquitous connectivity, how organizations collect, handle, and store user information is being closely scrutinized. Data privacy laws and compliance obligations are constantly changing, creating a challenging landscape for businesses to navigate. This section provides you with the knowledge you need to understand and comply with data privacy regulations.

9.1.1 Understanding the Data Privacy Landscape

Before getting into Data Privacy, It is important to understand what constitutes "personal data" or "personally identifiable information" (PII). Personal data refers to any information that can be used to identify an individual, either directly or indirectly. This includes obvious identifiers like names, addresses, and social security numbers, but can also encompass other data points like IP addresses, geolocation data, biometric information, and unique identifiers like cookie IDs. PII is a subset of personal data that can be used to identify, contact, or locate a specific individual. Examples of PII include full names, national identification numbers, financial account details, precise geolocation coordinates, and biometric records like fingerprints or facial recognition data.

Data privacy laws aim to protect this personal data and PII by regulating how it is collected, used, shared, and secured by organizations. The data privacy landscape varies around the world, but some key regulations have a global impact. Here are some prominent examples:

- **General Data Protection Regulation (GDPR):** The GDPR is a regulation in EU law that governs data protection and privacy in the European Union (EU) and the European Economic Area. It also addresses the transfer of personal data outside of the EU and EEA regions. The GDPR applies to any organization that processes personal data from individuals residing in the EU, regardless of its location.

- **California Consumer Privacy Act (CCPA):** The California Consumer Privacy Act (CCPA) is a law that grants California residents the right to know about, access, and delete personal data collected by businesses. It also gives them the option to opt out of the sale of their personal information.

- **Health Insurance Portability and Accountability Act (HIPAA):** HIPAA is a US federal law that safeguards sensitive patient health information. It establishes the requirements for how covered entities (such as healthcare providers, health plans, and healthcare clearinghouses) must protect this information.

These are just a few examples; there are numerous other data privacy laws and regulations in effect around the world. Understanding which regulations apply to your organization based on its location, data collection methods, and usage is critical.

9.1.2 Key Aspects of Data Privacy Laws

Most data privacy laws share some common core principles:

- **Transparency:** Organizations must disclose what data they collect, how it is used, and with whom it is shared. This frequently entails implementing clear and concise privacy policies that inform users of their rights.

- **Individual Rights:** Data privacy laws frequently grant individuals control over their personal information. These rights may include the ability to access, correct, erase, and restrict the processing of their data. Organizations must establish procedures to allow individuals to exercise these rights.

- **Data Security:** Data privacy laws typically require organizations to put in place appropriate technical and organizational safeguards to protect personal information from unauthorized access, disclosure, alteration, or destruction. This could include things like encryption, access controls, and security awareness training.

9.1.3 Compliance Strategies

To navigate the complexities of data privacy laws, your organization can adopt the following key strategies:

- **Conduct a Data Inventory:** Identify the data you collect, where it is stored, and how it is used. This helps you determine which data privacy laws may apply to your organization.

- **Develop a Data Privacy Policy:** Create a clear and comprehensive data privacy policy that describes your data collection practices, how you use the data, and individuals' rights to their personal data.

- **Implement Data Security Measures:** Create a clear and comprehensive data privacy policy that describes your data collection practices, how you use the data, and individuals' rights to their personal data.

- **Train Employees on Data Privacy:** Educate your employees on data privacy best practices and make sure they understand their responsibilities when handling data.

- **Develop a Data Breach Response Plan:** Prepare an effective response plan for data breaches. This should include procedures for notifying affected parties and regulatory authorities.

Understanding the data privacy landscape, following relevant regulations, and implementing strong data security measures can help you reduce legal risks, build trust with your stakeholders, and foster a data privacy culture within your organization.

The road to data privacy compliance is an ongoing one. Keeping up with changing regulations and adapting your practices accordingly is critical for navigating this complex but necessary aspect of data security in today's digital world.

9.2 Innovative Data Protection and Encryption Strategies

In today's digital landscape, where data breaches and cyberattacks are constant threats, organizations must implement strong data protection strategies to protect sensitive information. Encryption is an important part of this data security strategy, but it is not the only tool in the arsenal. This section looks at new approaches to data protection and encryption that can help you secure your valuable data.

9.2.1 Beyond Traditional Encryption: Exploring Advanced Techniques

Encryption remains a critical component of data security, scrambling data to render it unreadable without a decryption key. However, along with traditional encryption methods, several innovative techniques are emerging to strengthen data security:

- **Homomorphic Encryption:** This advanced encryption technique enables computations to be performed directly on encrypted data without requiring decryption. This eliminates the need to decrypt sensitive data for processing, greatly lowering the risk of exposure.

- **Tokenization:** Tokenization replaces sensitive data (such as credit card numbers) with unique identifiers (tokens). These tokens have no inherent value and can only be decrypted into the original data through a separate process. This approach reduces the amount of sensitive data stored in systems, lowering the risk of a security breach.

- **Data Masking:** Data masking is the process of obscuring portions of sensitive information, such as Social Security numbers or email addresses. This technique enables authorized users to work with data for specific purposes while maintaining the confidentiality of all information.

- **Attribute-Based Encryption (ABE):** ABE provides access control based on user attributes rather than a single decryption key. This gives you more granular control over who can access specific data based on their roles or permissions within the organization.

These innovative techniques, combined with traditional encryption, provide a layered approach to data protection, providing increased security and flexibility for a variety of data security requirements.

9.2.2 Utilizing Data Loss Prevention (DLP) for Comprehensive Protection

Data Loss Prevention (DLP) is a security technology that enables organizations to detect, monitor, and control the movement of sensitive data. DLP systems can be set up to detect and prevent unauthorized data transfers, whether intentional or accidental. Here's how DLP improves data security:

- **Content Inspection:** DLP systems can look for specific keywords, patterns, or data types that indicate sensitive information. This enables the proactive identification of potential data breaches.

- **Data Classification:** DLP can be used to classify data according to its sensitivity level. This classification enables organizations to prioritize security measures and impose stricter controls on highly sensitive data.

- **Data Encryption:** DLP can be combined with encryption software to automatically encrypt sensitive data at rest or in transit. This provides an additional layer of protection for data, even if it violates DLP protocols.

Organizations can create a comprehensive defense against data exfiltration and unauthorized data disclosure by implementing DLP in conjunction with other data protection strategies.

9.2.3 Leveraging Cloud-Based Data Protection Services

Cloud computing provides a flexible and scalable solution for data storage and management. However, it is critical to secure data stored in the cloud. Cloud-based data protection services offer a variety of features to protect your information:

- **Cloud Key Management:** These services provide secure storage and access control for the encryption keys used to protect data in the cloud. This ensures that only authorized users or applications can decrypt and access sensitive information.

- **Data Residency and Compliance:** Cloud providers provide data residency options that ensure your data remains in specific geographic locations in order to comply with applicable data privacy regulations.

Using cloud-based data protection services can simplify data security management and ensure compliance with data privacy regulations, particularly for organizations that rely heavily on cloud storage.

Organizations can establish a strong data security posture in today's ever-changing threat landscape by combining innovative encryption techniques, data loss prevention tools, and cloud-based data protection services.

9.3 Assuring Data Integrity and Safeguarding Confidentiality

Data integrity and confidentiality are fundamental concepts in data security. Data integrity ensures that information is unaltered and trustworthy, whereas confidentiality safeguards sensitive data against unauthorized access and disclosure. This section delves into the best practices for achieving both of these objectives.

9.3.1 Maintaining Data Integrity

Data integrity ensures that data is consistent, accurate, and reliable throughout its entire lifecycle, from creation to storage and use. Here are key strategies for ensuring data integrity:

- **Access Controls:** Implementing strong access controls prevents data from being modified without authorization. This entails granting users and applications the bare minimum of access privileges necessary to complete their tasks.

- **Data Validation and Verification:** Validating and verifying data on a regular basis aids in the detection and correction of errors or inconsistencies that could jeopardize integrity. This can include data cleansing and checksum verification techniques.

- **Audit Trails and Logging:** Maintaining comprehensive audit trails and logs allows you to track data access and modifications. This enables the detection of unauthorized changes and the reconstruction of events in the event of a security breach.

- **Hashing:** Hashing functions create unique mathematical fingerprints for data. Any changes to the data produce a different hash value, making data tampering easy to detect.

Implementing these practices allows organizations to ensure the accuracy and trustworthiness of their data, fostering better decision making and mitigating the risks associated with corrupt or inaccurate information.

9.3.2 Safeguarding Data Confidentiality

Confidentiality ensures that sensitive information is only available to authorized users and applications. Here are some important measures to ensure data confidentiality:

- Encryption scrambles data with a cryptographic key, rendering it unreadable to those without it. This protects data both at rest (stored on devices) and in transit (transmitted across networks).

- Prioritizing security measures through data classification based on sensitivity level. Highly confidential data may necessitate stricter controls than less sensitive data.

- Minimizing data for business purposes reduces the risk of a breach and sensitive information exposure.

- Regular Security Awareness Training: Educating employees on data security best practices helps prevent social engineering attacks and phishing attempts that could compromise confidential data.

Implementing data confidentiality measures can significantly reduce the risk of unauthorized access to sensitive information while also protecting data privacy.

9.3.3 Achieving a Balance Between Data Security and Usability

Finding a balance between strong data security and usability is critical. Overly complex security measures can jeopardize productivity and user experience. Here are some strategies for achieving this balance:

- **Usable Authentication Methods:** Use secure and user-friendly multifactor authentication methods such as fingerprint scanners or one-time passwords.

- **Data Encryption with Transparency:** Use encryption solutions that are transparent to users to ensure data security without compromising user experience.

- **Security Automation:** Automate routine security tasks such as data encryption and access control management to reduce user workload while maintaining a strong security posture.

Organizations can develop a data security strategy that effectively protects information while allowing users to work more efficiently by carefully considering both security and usability.

Finally, by following these practices for ensuring data integrity and confidentiality, organizations can establish a strong data security framework that fosters trust, protects sensitive information, and reduces the risks associated with data breaches and unauthorized access.

CHAPTER 10

Proactive Intrusion Detection and Network Surveillance

This chapter focuses on proactive intrusion detection and network surveillance, both of which are critical components of a strong cybersecurity posture. As networks become more complex and cyber threats evolve at a rapid pace, traditional reactive security measures are insufficient. This chapter teaches you how to implement proactive strategies for identifying and mitigating security threats before they cause significant damage. We'll look at deploying Intrusion Detection Systems (IDS) and Intrusion Prevention Systems (IPS) for real-time threat response, as well as using Security Information and Event Management (SIEM) systems to get a centralized view of security events across your network. We'll look at techniques for analyzing network traffic to detect anomalies that could indicate potential intrusions. Understanding and implementing these proactive detection and surveillance methods will significantly improve your organization's ability to prevent cyberattacks and protect your valuable data and resources.

© The Editor(s) (if applicable) and The Author(s), under exclusive license to APress Media, LLC, part of Springer Nature 2024
S. Lekkala and P. Gurijala, *Security and Privacy for Modern Networks*, https://doi.org/10.1007/979-8-8688-0823-4_10

10.1 Deploying IDS and IPS for Real-Time Threat Response

Intrusion Detection Systems (IDS) and Intrusion Prevention Systems (IPS) are essential tools for an organization's proactive network security strategy. While they may sound similar, these systems serve different functions in protecting your network from unauthorized access and malicious activity. This section looks at their capabilities and deployment strategies for effective real-time threat response.

10.1.1 Intrusion Detection Systems (IDS): Sentinels of Network Security

An IDS functions as a network security sniffer, constantly monitoring network traffic for unusual activity that could indicate a potential intrusion attempt. Here's an explanation of how IDS works:

- **Signature-Based Detection:** IDS frequently rely on predefined signatures, which are basically patterns or fingerprints of known malicious activity. When the IDS detects traffic that matches a signature in its database, it issues an alert, informing security personnel of a potential threat.

- **Anomaly-Based Detection:** Advanced IDS can also use anomaly-based detection methods. These techniques examine network traffic patterns to detect deviations from normal baseline behavior. Deviations could indicate suspicious activity that does not necessarily match a known signature.

10.1.2 Intrusion Prevention Systems (IPS): Taking Action Against Threats

An IPS takes a more proactive approach than an IDS. An IPS can not only identify threats but also actively prevent them from infiltrating your network. Here is how IPS works:

- **Real-Time Threat Prevention:** When an IPS detects suspicious activity that matches a signature or deviates from normal behavior patterns, it can block malicious traffic, terminate connections, or quarantine infected devices. This quick response helps to contain threats and keep them from causing harm.

- **Deployment Strategies:** IPS are typically installed at strategic points on your network, such as firewalls or network gateways. This positioning enables them to monitor and filter all incoming and outgoing traffic.

10.1.3 Choosing the Right Tool: IDS vs. IPS

The choice between IDS and IPS depends on your specific security needs:

- **IDS:** Ideal for situations where you need to prioritize threat detection and analysis without having to block traffic. This allows for a better understanding of attacker behavior and more precise security measures.

- **IPS:** Better suited to environments where immediate threat prevention is essential. Using IPS can automatically shut down intrusions before they cause significant damage.

101

Combined Functionality

Some security solutions combine IDS and IPS functionality, allowing for detection and prevention on a single platform. This integrated approach can simplify security management while providing a comprehensive defense against cyberattacks.

10.1.4 Enhancing Threat Response with IDS/IPS

To improve the effectiveness of IDS and IPS in real-time threat response:

- **Maintain Updated Threat Signatures:** Regularly update your IDS/IPS signatures to ensure they can detect the most recent threats and vulnerabilities.

- **Fine-Tune Anomaly Detection:** Calibrate anomaly detection settings to reduce false positives (alerts caused by harmless activity) while remaining sensitive to real threats.

- **Establish Response Procedures:** Create clear incident response procedures to handle alerts generated by IDS/IPS. This ensures a timely and coordinated response to security incidents.

By strategically deploying and effectively maintaining IDS and IPS, you can significantly improve your organization's ability to identify and respond to security threats in real time, defending your network against cyberattacks and protecting your valuable data assets.

10.2 Utilizing SIEM for Enhanced Security Oversight

Security Information and Event Management (SIEM) systems are critical for gaining a unified view of security events across your network. In today's complex IT environments, SIEM serves as a command center for security operations, consolidating and analyzing data from multiple security tools. This section looks at how SIEM provides organizations with improved security oversight and threat detection capabilities.

10.2.1 Centralized Logging and Event Correlation

Traditional security solutions frequently produce a large number of logs and security events from firewalls, IDS/IPS, endpoints, and other tools. These logs are dispersed across multiple systems, making it difficult to detect and investigate security incidents effectively. SIEM systems tackle this issue by

- **Centralized Log Collection:** SIEM serves as a central repository for security logs and events generated by various network and security devices. This consolidated view improves log management and simplifies security analysis.

- **Event Correlation:** SIEM goes beyond just collecting logs. It uses powerful correlation rules to analyze these events and detect potential security incidents. Correlation rules can detect patterns or sequences of events that suggest a coordinated attack or suspicious activity.

10.2.2 Threat Detection and Incident Response

Using centralized logging and event correlation, SIEM enables security teams to

- **Improve Threat Detection:** SIEM's ability to correlate events from multiple sources enables earlier detection of potential threats. Correlations can reveal hidden patterns that individual security tools operating independently may miss.

- **Streamline Incident Response:** When a security incident is detected, SIEM provides a consolidated view of the event, which includes relevant logs and data from multiple security tools. This centralized perspective allows security teams to respond to incidents faster and more efficiently.

10.2.3 Security Information and Event Management (SIEM) Features

SIEM solutions offer a range of functionalities to enhance security oversight:

- **Real-Time Monitoring:** Many SIEM systems include dashboards that show security events and potential threats as they happen. This enables security analysts to keep track of ongoing activity and detect emerging threats quickly.

- **Compliance Reporting:** SIEM can produce reports demonstrating your organization's adherence to security regulations and compliance standards. These reports can be extremely useful during security audits.

- **User Activity Monitoring (UAM):** SIEM can work with User Entity and Behavior Analytics (UEBA) tools to track user behavior across the network. This allows for the detection of unusual user behavior, which may indicate compromised accounts or insider threats.

10.2.4 Selecting and Implementing a SIEM Solution

Choosing the right SIEM solution depends on your organization's specific needs and security infrastructure. Here are some key factors to consider:

- Scalability: Ensure the SIEM solution can handle the volume of logs and events generated by your network.

- Ensure SIEM integrates seamlessly with existing security tools and infrastructure.

- Security Analytics: Assess SIEM's ability to correlate events and detect threats.

By successfully implementing a SIEM solution, you can gain a comprehensive view of your security posture, identify and respond to threats more quickly, and improve your overall security incident response capabilities.

10.3 Analyzing Network Traffic to Identify Anomalies

In the ever-changing landscape of cyber threats, organizations need reliable methods to detect malicious activity on their networks. Analyzing network traffic for anomalies, or deviations from usual patterns, is a critical technique for detecting potential security incidents. This section discusses the strategies and considerations for identifying anomalies in network traffic data.

10.3.1 Establishing a Baseline for Normal Traffic

Understanding what constitutes "normal" network traffic for your organization is the first step in anomaly detection. Here's how to set a baseline:

- Traffic Monitoring: Continuously monitor network traffic patterns, such as data volume, packet size distribution, protocol usage, and source-destination communication flows.

- Time-based analysis involves examining traffic patterns over time to identify trends and seasonal variations. Weekday traffic patterns may differ significantly from weekends, for example.

- Identify authorized users and devices on your network. This helps to distinguish between legitimate and unauthorized traffic.

By gaining a thorough understanding of normal network behavior, you can establish benchmarks for detecting significant deviations that could indicate potential security threats.

10.3.2 Anomaly Detection Techniques

Once you have a baseline, you can employ various techniques to detect anomalies in network traffic:

- **Statistical Anomaly Detection:** This method examines the statistical properties of traffic data, such as the mean, median, and standard deviation. Significant deviations from these expected values may indicate anomalies.

- **Machine Learning-Based Anomaly Detection:**
  Machine learning algorithms can be trained on
  historical network traffic data to identify typical
  patterns. Deviations from these patterns can then be
  flagged by the model as potential anomalies.

Choosing the Right Technique

The best anomaly detection technique depends on your specific
requirements and the complexity of your network traffic. Statistical
methods are simpler, whereas machine learning can perform more
sophisticated analyses but requires a larger data set for training.

10.3.3 Challenges of Anomaly Detection

Network traffic anomaly detection presents certain challenges:

- **False Positives:** Anomaly detection systems can issue
  alerts for minor deviations from the baseline.
  Fine-tuning detection algorithms and incorporating
  threat intelligence can help to reduce false positives.

- **Evolving Threats:** Anomaly detection systems can
  generate alerts for minor deviations from the baseline.
  Fine-tuning detection algorithms and incorporating
  threat intelligence can aid in reducing false positives.

10.3.4 Benefits of Network Traffic Anomaly Detection

Despite the challenges, network traffic anomaly detection offers significant
benefits:

- **Early Threat Detection:** By identifying anomalies, you can detect potential security incidents in their early stages, allowing for faster response and mitigation before they cause significant damage.

- **Improved Security Posture:** Network traffic anomaly detection strengthens your overall security posture by proactively identifying suspicious activity that might evade traditional signature-based security solutions.

Understanding the techniques, challenges, and benefits of network traffic anomaly detection enables you to use this valuable tool to improve your organization's cybersecurity efforts and protect your network from evolving threats.

CHAPTER 11

Secure Connectivity with Virtual Private Networks

As the digital world expands and our reliance on remote access grows, securing our online activities becomes increasingly important. This chapter delves into the world of Virtual Private Networks (VPNs), a fundamental technology for establishing secure connections over public networks. Consider a secure, encrypted tunnel spanning the vast expanse of the Internet. This tunnel, which a VPN creates, protects your data transmissions from prying eyes and possible interception. This chapter teaches you how to harness the power of VPNs. We'll look at the various VPN protocols and their security features, allowing you to choose the best solution for your needs. We'll look at how to effectively manage and deploy VPNs to ensure that your workforce has seamless and secure remote access. Whether you're a telecommuter connecting to your company's network or a traveler looking for secure Wi-Fi access in a public hotspot, understanding VPNs allows you to navigate the online world with confidence, knowing that your communications are protected from unauthorized access. By the end of this chapter, you'll be able to use VPNs as an important tool in your cybersecurity arsenal, protecting your data privacy and ensuring secure connectivity in today's dynamic digital environment.

© The Editor(s) (if applicable) and The Author(s), under exclusive license to APress Media, LLC, part of Springer Nature 2024
S. Lekkala and P. Gurijala, *Security and Privacy for Modern Networks*,
https://doi.org/10.1007/979-8-8688-0823-4_11

11.1 Understanding VPN Protocols and Their Security Features

Virtual Private Networks (VPNs) provide a powerful way to secure your online communications. A VPN encrypts your data traffic and establishes a secure connection between your device and a remote server. This encryption protects your data from eavesdropping, even when you use public Wi-Fi networks or untrusted Internet connections. However, with numerous VPN protocols available, understanding their functionalities and security features is critical for selecting the best option for your requirements.

11.1.1 VPN Protocols: The Language of Secure Tunnels

VPN protocols specify the rules and algorithms that govern how data is encapsulated, transmitted, and secured within the VPN tunnel. Let's take a closer look at some common VPN protocols.

- **Point-to-Point Tunneling Protocol (PPTP):** An older and widely used protocol, PPTP is simple to use but uses weaker encryption standards, making it less secure for sensitive data.

- **Layer 2 Tunneling Protocol (L2TP):** When combined with stronger encryption protocols such as IPSec, L2TP provides superior security to PPTP. However, L2TP itself does not offer encryption.

- **SSL/TLS:** These protocols are widely used to secure website connections (HTTPS). VPN solutions can also use SSL/TLS to ensure secure data transmission within the VPN tunnel.

- **OpenVPN:** This is an open source protocol known for its robust encryption, flexibility, and customization options. OpenVPN provides a high level of security but may necessitate more technical knowledge to set up.

11.1.2 Security Features: Choosing the Right Armor for Your VPN

When selecting a VPN protocol, consider the following security features, which serve as armor protecting your data within the VPN tunnel:

- **Encryption Strength:** The level of encryption used to protect your data while in the VPN tunnel. Stronger encryption algorithms provide better protection, but they may reduce performance.

- **Authentication Methods:** The methods used to confirm the identities of users and VPN servers prior to establishing a secure connection. Strong authentication methods ensure that only authorized users and trusted servers have access to the VPN.

- **Data Integrity:** Mechanisms to ensure that data transmitted through the VPN tunnel is not tampered with during transit. Data integrity features ensure that the data you receive is identical to the data that was sent.

Understanding the available VPN protocols and their security features allows you to make informed decisions about which solution best balances security requirements, performance, and ease of use for your specific needs. The following sections of this chapter will go over effective VPN deployment strategies and solutions for secure remote access.

11.2 Effective Management and Deployment of VPNs

After discussing the technical foundations of VPN protocols in the previous section, we will now look at the critical aspects of effective VPN management and deployment. This ensures your workforce has seamless and secure remote access, allowing them to work productively from anywhere.

11.2.1 Planning and Design: Building the Foundation for Secure Remote Access

A successful VPN deployment requires meticulous planning and design. Here's a breakdown of key considerations for building a strong foundation:

- **User and Access Management**

  - **Identify Authorized Users:** Determine which employees need remote access through VPN. This helps to limit access to only those who really need it.

  - **Define Access Privileges:** Create granular access controls. Do not grant blanket access. Instead, define permissions based on user roles and responsibilities. For example, a sales representative may only require access to customer relationship management (CRM) software, whereas a network administrator may require complete access to network devices and configurations. This reduces the potential harm if a malicious actor gains unauthorized access.

- **Deployment Options:** Decide between deploying a remote access VPN solution on-premises or utilizing a cloud-based VPN service.

  - **On-Premises VPN Deployment**

    - **Advantages:** Provides greater control over the VPN infrastructure and security posture, allowing for customization to meet your specific requirements.

    - **Disadvantages:** To ensure ongoing management, a significant investment in hardware, software, and IT expertise is required. Scalability can be challenging as the number of remote users increases, potentially necessitating additional infrastructure investment.

  - **Cloud-Based VPN Service**

    - **Advantages:** Easy to set up and manage, requiring little hardware and software investment on your part. Scalability is often automatic, allowing for an increasing number of remote users.

    - **Disadvantages:** Security considerations are critical because you are entrusting the cloud provider with your data traffic. Assess the provider's security practices, data residency policies, and compliance certifications to ensure they are consistent with your organization's security posture.

- **Network Infrastructure:** Make sure your network infrastructure is capable of handling the increased traffic load caused by VPN connections. This may involve:

  - **Upgrading Bandwidth:** Increased data flow due to VPN usage might necessitate a bandwidth upgrade to maintain acceptable performance.

  - **Network Segmentation:** Implement network segmentation to isolate VPN traffic. This creates separate zones for VPN users, restricting their access to only authorized resources and minimizing the security risks associated with compromised devices. For example, a segment can be created specifically for VPN users, separating them from the internal network that houses critical servers and databases. Network segmentation helps contain the potential impact of a security breach.

11.2.2 Configuration and Implementation: Bringing the VPN to Life

With a well-defined plan in place, you can move forward with the configuration and implementation phase.

- **Server Configuration:** Configure the VPN server with the appropriate protocol (PPTP, L2TP/IPsec, OpenVPN, etc.) and security settings. This includes defining

  - **User Authentication Methods:** Select strong authentication methods such as multifactor authentication (MFA), which go beyond simple username and password combinations. MFA provides an additional layer of security by requiring a second verification factor, such as a code from an authenticator app on the user's smartphone.

- **Encryption Algorithms:** Use strong encryption algorithms like AES-256 to scramble data transmissions within the VPN tunnel, making them unintelligible even if intercepted.

- **Access Controls:** Define the allowed IP addresses and network resources that authorized VPN users can access. This fine-grained control helps to limit access to sensitive data.

- **Client Deployment:** Distribute and install VPN client software to authorized user devices (computers, smartphones, tablets). Provide users with clear instructions for configuring and connecting to the VPN, ensuring proper authentication and secure access.

  - **Testing and Validation:** Conduct thorough testing of the VPN deployment to ensure

    - **Secure Connectivity:** Users can successfully establish secure connections to the VPN server.

    - **Performance:** VPN connections provide acceptable connection speeds for the intended use cases. There should be no significant degradation in performance when compared to non-VPN connections.

    - **Compatibility:** The VPN client software functions correctly on different devices and operating systems used by your workforce.

11.2.3 Ongoing Management and Maintenance: Keeping Your VPN Secure

Ongoing management and maintenance are required to keep a VPN deployment secure and healthy.

- **Security Patch Management:** To address vulnerabilities and prevent exploits used by malicious actors, update VPN server and client software on a regular basis with the most recent security patches.

- **User Management:** Add, remove, and modify user access privileges as needed to ensure security and compliance. User access should be reviewed on a regular basis to ensure it is consistent with current roles and responsibilities.

- **Monitoring and Logging:** Keep an eye on VPN activity for signs of suspicious behavior, such as unusual login attempts or data exfiltration. Implement logging.

- **Monitoring and Logging (continued):** Implement logging to track VPN connection attempts, user activity, and disconnections. This log data can be used for auditing, which aids in the detection and investigation of potential security incidents.

- **User Training:** Provide regular security awareness training to users on best practices for using the VPN. This training should cover topics like

    - Identifying phishing attacks that try to steal VPN credentials.

- Avoiding using public Wi-Fi for sensitive activities without a VPN connection.

- Reporting any suspicious activity or security concerns regarding the VPN.

By implementing these VPN deployment and management strategies, you can provide secure remote access to your workforce while protecting your organization's sensitive information. Remember that while a VPN is an effective tool, it is only one component of a comprehensive security strategy. A layered security approach that includes strong passwords, multifactor authentication, endpoint security solutions, and user education is required to build a strong defense against cyber threats.

11.3 Solutions for Secure and Flexible Remote Access

Virtual Private Networks (VPNs) are an effective solution for secure remote access, but they are not the only option. This section looks at complementary solutions that provide flexibility while also addressing some of VPN's limitations.

11.3.1 Beyond VPNs: Expanding the Remote Access Toolkit

While VPNs are a critical component of secure remote access, there are some situations where alternative solutions may be more appropriate. Here are some more options to consider:

- **Zero-Trust Network Access (ZTNA):** A relatively novel approach to remote access that departs from the traditional network perimeter model. ZTNA grants access based on the "least privilege" principle, which limits access to authorized users and the specific resources they require, regardless of their location. This approach may be more secure and dynamic than VPNs, particularly for cloud-based applications.

- **Remote Desktop Protocol (RDP) and Virtual Network Computing (VNC):** These protocols allow for direct control of a remote computer via a network connection. RDP is a proprietary Microsoft protocol commonly used for Windows desktops, whereas VNC provides platform-independent remote access functionality. However, RDP and VNC frequently necessitate complex firewall configurations and strong passwords to reduce security risks. Two-factor authentication should be required for RDP/VNC connections.

- **Cloud-Based Access Solutions:** Cloud service providers provide direct access to applications and desktops via a web browser, eliminating the need for a VPN connection. This simplifies remote access for users while reducing the burden on IT to manage remote access infrastructure. However, security concerns are paramount when using cloud-based solutions, as user data is stored on the cloud provider's servers.

11.3.2 Choosing the Right Solution: A Multipronged Approach

The best remote access solution is based on your specific needs and security requirements. Here are some factors to consider when making your decision:

- **Security Requirements:** The level of security required for the data being accessed. ZTNA and strong two-factor authentication provide better security than traditional VPNs.

- **User Requirements:** The level of access that users require (complete desktop control, application access, file sharing). RDP/VNC is appropriate for full desktop control, whereas cloud-based solutions may be preferable for specific applications.

- **Ease of Use and Manageability:** IT resources are available to manage and maintain the remote access solution. Cloud-based solutions are typically easier to manage than on-premises solutions such as VPNs.

- **Scalability:** The need to support an increasing number of remote users. Cloud-based solutions are typically more scalable than on-premises solutions.

11.3.3 Conclusion: Building a Comprehensive Remote Access Strategy

A secure and flexible remote access strategy frequently combines solutions rather than relying on a single tool. Understanding the strengths and limitations of VPNs, ZTNA, RDP/VNC, and cloud-based access solutions allows you to design a multilayered approach that meets a wide range of user requirements while maintaining strong security. To protect your organization's data in a remote work environment, prioritize strong authentication methods, keep software up to date, and educate users on cybersecurity best practices.

CHAPTER 12

Securing Networks with SDN and SD-WAN

As we continue our investigation into effective security and privacy strategies for modern networks, we reach a critical chapter that focuses on Software-Defined Networking (SDN) and SD-WAN. These innovative technologies are reshaping network management and security paradigms. This chapter examines how SDN and SD-WAN can improve network security by introducing centralized control, dynamic policy enforcement, and better data protection mechanisms.

12.1 Introduction to SDN and SD-WAN for Enhanced Security

The constantly evolving threat landscape necessitates ongoing improvement of network security strategies. This section discusses Software-Defined Networking (SDN) and SD-WAN (Software-Defined Wide Area Network), two innovative technologies that are transforming network management and security paradigms. SDN and SD-WAN

S. Lekkala and P. Gurijala, *Security and Privacy for Modern Networks*, https://doi.org/10.1007/979-8-8688-0823-4_12

outperform traditional networking approaches in terms of security because they decouple control and data planes and centralize network management.

12.1.1 The Shift from Traditional Networking to SDN/SD-WAN

Traditional networking uses static configurations and hardware-based control planes. This approach makes it difficult to respond to evolving security threats and network demands. SDN and SD-WAN mark a fundamental shift in networking:

- **Software-Defined Networking (SDN):** In physical and virtual networks, the control plane (network intelligence) and data plane (data forwarding) are separated, disrupting the traditional model. This separation permits

  - **Centralized Network Management:** Network administrators can configure and manage network devices from a single location, which simplifies network operations and enforces security policies.

  - **Programmable Network Security:** SDN enables the development of automated security policies and dynamic responses to security incidents, thereby increasing overall network agility.

- **SD-WAN (Software-Defined Wide Area Network):** SD-WAN centralizes the management and optimization of geographically dispersed WAN connections. This provides

- **Improved Visibility and Control:** SD-WAN provides a comprehensive view of all WAN connections, giving you greater control over traffic routing and security measures.

- **Dynamic Traffic Optimization:** SD-WAN can intelligently choose the most secure and efficient data path based on real-time network conditions and security concerns.

12.1.2 Key Security Challenges Addressed by SDN and SD-WAN

Traditional network security faces numerous challenges due to the limitations of hardware-based control planes and static configurations. SDN and SD-WAN provide solutions to the following limitations:

- **Complex Manual Configurations:** Traditional networking frequently relies on manual configuration of individual network devices, which is error-prone and time-consuming. Configuration management is automated using SDN and SD-WAN, reducing human error and ensuring security policy consistency and enables automated security response and remediation.

- **Inconsistent Security Policies:** Maintaining consistent security policies across a complex network of disparate devices can be difficult in traditional configurations. SDN and SD-WAN enable centralized policy management, ensuring that security controls are applied consistently across the network.

- **Limited Visibility into Network Traffic:** Traditional networks may provide limited visibility into data flows, making it difficult to detect and respond to security threats. SDN and SD-WAN enhance network visibility, allowing for comprehensive traffic monitoring and threat detection.

- **Segmentation and Access Control:** Segmentation allows for the network to be divided into smaller subnets. Each network segment acts as its own network which enables security teams to have more control over the traffic by implementing segment-specific access control mechanisms.

SDN and SD-WAN address these challenges, laying the groundwork for a more secure and adaptable network security posture. The following sections will go into greater detail about the specific security enhancements provided by these innovative technologies.

12.2 Core Security Enhancements with SDN and SD-WAN

SDN and SD-WAN provide significant advantages over traditional networking approaches, particularly in terms of security. This section looks at how these technologies achieve centralized control and policy enforcement, resulting in a more secure network environment.

12.2.1 Centralized Control and Policy Enforcement

One of the most significant security advantages of SDN and SD-WAN is their ability to centralize control and policy enforcement. By separating the control plane from the data plane, these technologies allow network administrators to manage security policies from a single point of control. This provides several advantages:

- **Simplified Security Management:** Administrators can define and enforce security policies for the entire network from a centralized location. This eliminates the need to manually configure each device, reducing complexity and the risk of human error.

- **Rapid Security Response:** Centralized control enables quicker and more coordinated responses to security incidents. Security teams can quickly detect threats and implement mitigation strategies across the entire network.

- **Scalability and Consistency:** As networks expand and evolve, centralized policy management ensures that security controls are consistently applied to all devices and locations. This eliminates any security gaps that may exist in traditional, distributed management approaches.

The following sections go into greater detail about how centralized control and policy enforcement contribute to improved network security:

Streamlined Network Monitoring and Response

SDN and SD-WAN offer a centralized view of network traffic, allowing for comprehensive network monitoring and faster detection of security threats. Here's how:

- **Real-Time Network Visibility:** SDN and SD-WAN provide real-time visibility into network activity, allowing administrators to detect suspicious traffic patterns and potential security threats.

- **Automated Threat Detection:** Centralized network intelligence enables the implementation of automated threat detection mechanisms. These systems can analyze network traffic in real time and send alerts when they detect suspicious activity.

- **Faster Incident Response:** Centralized control enables faster response to security incidents. Security teams can quickly identify threats, quarantine infected devices, and implement mitigation strategies to reduce damage.

SDN and SD-WAN enable security teams to identify and respond to security threats more proactively by streamlining network monitoring and response.

Consistent Security Policy Across the Network

In traditional configurations, it can be difficult to maintain consistent security policies across a complex network with many devices. SDN and SD-WAN tackle this issue by

- **Centralized Policy Definition:** Security policies are defined and enforced from a single location to ensure consistency across all network devices and locations.

- **Automated Policy Enforcement:** SDN and SD-WAN automate security policy enforcement, reducing the risk of human error and ensuring that security controls are applied consistently.

- **Dynamic Policy Updates:** Centralized management enables security policies to be dynamically updated in response to evolving threats or changes in network configuration.

Consistent security policy enforcement across the entire network reduces security vulnerabilities and the attack surface that malicious actors can exploit.

12.2.2 Secure Connectivity and Data Protection

Beyond centralized control, SDN and SD-WAN provide significant improvements in data protection and secure communication channels. This section investigates how these technologies protect data in transit across networks.

Encryption and Secure Tunneling in SD-WAN

Traditional WAN connections may lack robust security features, exposing data to interception. SD-WAN addresses this concern by using encryption and secure tunneling mechanisms.

- **Encryption:** SD-WAN can encrypt data traffic before sending it over WAN links. This encryption scrambles the data, making it unreadable to anyone without the decryption key. AES (Advanced Encryption Standard) and TLS (Transport Layer Security) are two commonly used encryption protocols in SD-WAN.

- **Secure Tunneling:** SD-WAN can create secure tunnels over public networks, such as the Internet. These tunnels serve as virtual encrypted pathways, ensuring that data remains confidential and secure from unauthorized access even when traveling across untrustworthy networks. IPsec (Internet Protocol Security) and GRE are two common tunneling protocols used in SD-WAN.

SD-WAN protects data privacy and integrity by utilizing encryption and secure tunneling, particularly when connecting to geographically dispersed WANs.

Dynamic Path Selection for Traffic Integrity

Traditional WANs may route data along predetermined paths, which can be less secure or prone to congestion. SD-WAN uses dynamic path selection to improve traffic integrity.

- **Real-Time Path Analysis:** SD-WAN can analyze network conditions in real time, including bandwidth availability, latency, and the security posture of available routes.

- **Dynamic Routing Based on Security:** Based on real-time analysis, SD-WAN can dynamically select the most secure and reliable data path. This could include prioritizing paths with strong encryption or avoiding congested or potentially compromised links.

- **Improved Resilience Against Denial-of-Service Attacks (DoS):** By dynamically selecting paths, SD-WAN can help mitigate DoS attacks on specific network links. SD-WAN complicates attackers' attempts to disrupt network operations by distributing traffic across multiple paths.

Dynamic path selection based on security considerations ensures that data travels along the most secure and reliable routes possible, lowering the risk of data breaches and improving overall network resilience.

12.3 Future Directions and Challenges in Network Security

SDN and SD-WAN provide significant security benefits, but the cybersecurity landscape is constantly changing. This section delves into critical considerations for the future of network security with the continued adoption of these innovative technologies:

12.3.1 Integrating Emerging Technologies for Advanced Threat Protection

The security landscape is constantly evolving, and network security must adapt to meet these changes. Here are some promising areas for integrating SDN and SD-WAN for advanced threat protection:

- **Security Information and Event Management (SIEM):** Integrating SIEM systems with SDN and SD-WAN can provide a complete picture of security events across the network. This allows for real-time threat correlation and faster response times.

- **Machine Learning (ML) and Artificial Intelligence (AI):** Using AI and ML can improve threat detection capabilities. SDN and SD-WAN can be combined with AI/ML systems to analyze network traffic in real time, detect anomalies, and predict security incidents.

- **Zero-Trust Network Access (ZTNA):** ZTNA is a security model that removes implicit trust from the network. SDN can be used to implement ZTNA principles by dynamically granting access to resources based on user identity and context, thereby reducing the attack surface.

Organizations can improve their security posture and respond to evolving threats more proactively by integrating these emerging technologies.

12.3.2 Balancing Performance with Security in Scalable Network Environments

As network environments become more complex and scalable, balancing performance with security becomes a critical challenge.

- **Resource Optimization:** Security controls may consume network resources. Finding the right balance is critical to ensuring that security measures do not significantly impair network performance or user experience.

- **Scalability of Security Solutions:** To meet increasing network demands, security solutions must be scalable. SDN can help by allowing for the orchestration and automated deployment of security controls across large network infrastructures.

- **Integration with Cloud Security:** With an increasing reliance on cloud-based resources, security must extend to the cloud environment. SDN and SD-WAN can help to integrate on-premises and cloud security solutions, resulting in a more holistic security posture.

Organizations can use SDN and SD-WAN to achieve a balance of robust security and optimal network performance in scalable environments by carefully considering these challenges and taking a strategic approach.

The future of network security is likely to include continuous innovation and integration with emerging technologies. Organizations can ensure that their networks are well-protected in the face of evolving threats by staying informed about these trends and adapting their security strategies accordingly.

To summarize, Software-Defined Networking (SDN) and SD-WAN (Software-Defined Wide Area Network) represent a paradigm shift in network security. These technologies provide significant advantages over traditional approaches by decoupling the control and data planes and centralizing network management. SDN and SD-WAN enable organizations to achieve centralized control and policy enforcement, simplify network monitoring and response, and ensure network-wide security. Additionally, encryption, secure tunneling, and dynamic path selection in SD-WAN improve data security. While the future will present challenges in integrating with emerging technologies and balancing security and performance in scalable environments, SDN and SD-WAN provide a solid foundation for developing secure and adaptable network security postures in the face of ever-changing threats.

CHAPTER 13

Establishing Robust Perimeter Defenses

Cyber threats are always present in today's vast digital world. This chapter teaches you how to build a strong perimeter defense mechanism for your network, which serves as the first line of defense against cyberattacks. We'll look at how firewalls, which act as gatekeepers for network traffic, work. We'll also go over best practices for strengthening these defense mechanisms and introduce Unified Threat Management (UTM) solutions, which are a comprehensive security suite that combines various security functions to provide holistic protection. By arming yourself with this knowledge, you will be able to protect your valuable data and resources in the ever-changing digital landscape.

13.1 Exploring Firewall Technologies and Their Capabilities

Firewalls serve as your network's gatekeepers, meticulously examining all incoming and outgoing data traffic. They operate according to a set of predefined security rules, allowing access to authorized traffic while blocking anything deemed malicious or suspicious. Understanding the various firewall technologies allows you to choose the most appropriate solution for your specific requirements. Here, we delve into three major firewall technologies.

S. Lekkala and P. Gurijala, *Security and Privacy for Modern Networks*, https://doi.org/10.1007/979-8-8688-0823-4_13

13.1.1 Packet Filtering Firewalls: The Traditional Guardians

Packet filtering firewalls, the workhorses of traditional network security, examine individual data packets. They examine each packet's source and destination IP addresses, port numbers, and protocols. Based on these criteria, the firewall either allows or denies passage. Packet filtering firewalls provide basic security, but they have the following limitations:

- **Inability to Detect Complex Threats:** They may struggle to identify sophisticated threats that manipulate packet characteristics to avoid detection.

- **Limited Context Awareness:** They fail to consider the context of network connections, leaving them vulnerable to techniques that exploit established connections.

While packet filtering firewalls provide a basic layer of security, they may be insufficient for effective defense in today's complex threat landscape.

13.1.2 Stateful Firewalls: Building on the Foundation

Stateful firewalls extend the capabilities of packet filtering firewalls by including stateful inspection. This means that they not only analyze individual packets, but also keep track of active network connections. Given this context, stateful firewalls can dynamically assess traffic flow and allow only packets from established connections. This provides significant security improvements over packet filtering firewalls, enabling them to

- **Identify Suspicious Activity:** Stateful firewalls can detect attempts to exploit existing connections or establish unauthorized connections from unexpected sources.

- **Enhance Security Posture:** This more granular control over traffic flow improves your network's overall security.

Stateful firewalls represent a significant advancement in firewall technology, providing a more comprehensive approach to network security.

13.1.3 Next-Generation Firewalls (NGFWs): The Vanguard of Network Security

Next-generation firewalls (NGFWs) are the leading edge of firewall technology. They combine the benefits of stateful inspection with a slew of advanced features, resulting in a formidable defense against modern cyber threats. NGFWs go beyond basic packet inspection, providing functionalities like

- **Deep Packet Inspection:** NGFWs go deeper, inspecting both the headers and the data payload of packets. This allows them to detect malware, zero-day threats, and other malicious content embedded in data streams.

- **Intrusion Detection and Prevention Systems (IDS/IPS):** Many NGFWs include IDS/IPS capabilities that detect and block malicious activity attempting to infiltrate your network.

When compared to traditional firewalls, NGFWs provide unparalleled protection due to their incorporation of advanced capabilities. They are ideal for organizations that need a strong defense against sophisticated cyberattacks.

13.2 Best Practices for Perimeter Defense Optimization

Firewalls are an important part of any security strategy, but they are not a magic bullet. Optimizing your perimeter defense necessitates a multilayered approach that extends beyond simply installing firewalls. Here, we look at key best practices for fortifying your defense mechanisms and building a strong shield against cyber threats.

13.2.1 Establish a Clear Security Policy

A well-defined security policy serves as the foundation for any successful security strategy. This policy specifies the acceptable network usage and access control procedures. A clear and comprehensive security policy serves as a guideline for configuring firewalls and other security measures, ensuring that everyone understands their role in maintaining a secure network. Here are some key elements that a security policy should cover:

- **Authorized Users and Access Levels:** Define who is authorized to access the network and what level of access they have. This helps to prevent unauthorized access attempts and reduces the potential damage from a breach.

- **Acceptable Use:** Specify what activities are acceptable and prohibited on the network. This includes restrictions on downloading unauthorized software, visiting malicious websites, and engaging in activities that may jeopardize network security.

- **Password Management:** Create strong password policies, such as minimum password length, complexity requirements, and regular password changes.

- **Incident Response Procedures:** Establish a clear process for identifying, reporting, and responding to security incidents. This ensures a prompt and coordinated response to security breaches, thereby reducing potential damage.

Establishing a clear security policy and effectively communicating it to all users will significantly improve your organization's overall security posture.

13.2.2 Maintain Vigilance: Regular Updates and Monitoring

Eternal vigilance is paramount in cybersecurity. Here are practices to ensure your defense mechanisms remain effective:

- **Keep Firewalls Updated:** Regularly update your firewall firmware with the most recent security patches. These patches address vulnerabilities that malicious actors may attempt to exploit. Outdated firmware can expose significant security vulnerabilities in your defense mechanisms.

- **Patch Management:** Implement a comprehensive patch management strategy to ensure that all network devices and software applications are updated with the most recent security patches. This includes the operating systems, applications, and firmware for all network devices.

- **Monitor Firewall Logs:** Regularly examine firewall logs for suspicious activity, potential security incidents, and attempts to circumvent security controls. Firewall logs provide useful information about network traffic patterns and potential security threats.

By taking a proactive approach to updates and monitoring, you can detect and address vulnerabilities before they are exploited by attackers.

13.2.3 Network Segmentation: Compartmentalizing Your Network

Network segmentation is the process of dividing your network into distinct segments, isolating critical systems and resources from untrusted networks and public Internet access. This approach provides several security advantages:

- **Limits Blast Radius:** If a breach occurs in one segment, the damage is limited to that segment, preventing attackers from easily accessing critical systems and resources in other segments.

- **Improves Security Management:** Network segmentation makes security management easier by allowing you to apply different security controls to different segments depending on their criticality.

Segmenting your network adds an extra layer of defense, making it more difficult for attackers to move laterally within your network and compromise sensitive assets.

Additional Best Practices

In addition to the practices mentioned above, consider implementing

- **User Awareness:** User awareness is critical. Educate your users on cybersecurity best practices, such as recognizing phishing attempts and avoiding risky browsing habits. Empowered users serve as the first line of defense against social engineering attacks.

- **Multifactor Authentication (MFA):** Implement MFA wherever possible. MFA adds an extra layer of security by requiring a second verification factor in addition to the username and password. This significantly reduces the risk of unauthorized access, even if attackers gain user credentials.

By following these best practices and remaining vigilant, you can improve the effectiveness of your perimeter defense mechanisms and create a more secure digital environment for your organization.

13.3 Integrating Unified Threat Management (UTM) Solutions

In today's constantly changing threat landscape, organizations require comprehensive security solutions that go beyond traditional firewalls. Unified Threat Management (UTM) solutions meet this need by combining multiple security features into a single appliance or software suite. This integrated approach provides several benefits, including simplified security management and a comprehensive view of your network's security posture.

13.3.1 Unveiling the Powerhouse: Core Functions of UTM Solutions

UTM solutions combine the capabilities of various security tools to provide a multilayered defense against cyber threats. Here's a breakdown of some core functionalities commonly included in UTM solutions:

- **Stateful Firewall:** A stateful firewall is the foundation of any UTM solution, inspecting incoming and outgoing network traffic and enforcing predefined security rules. It allows legitimate traffic while blocking anything considered malicious or suspicious.

- **Intrusion Detection/Prevention Systems (IDS/IPS):** UTM solutions frequently incorporate IDS/IPS capabilities. IDS constantly monitors network traffic for unusual activity, such as port scans, denial-of-service attacks (DoS), and other malicious attempts. IPS takes a more proactive approach, actively blocking such attacks to protect your network.

- **Antivirus and Anti-malware Protection:** UTM solutions can protect your network against viruses, malware, ransomware, and other malicious software threats. They typically use real-time threat intelligence to detect and prevent emerging threats at the network perimeter.

- **Content Filtering:** UTMs can filter web traffic and prevent access to malicious websites or those that violate your organization's security policies. This helps users avoid unintentionally downloading malware or visiting phishing websites.

- **Web Application Firewalls (WAFs):** Some UTM solutions may also include WAFs to protect web applications against attacks. WAFs can detect and prevent a variety of web application vulnerabilities, including SQL injection and cross-site scripting attacks.

Additional Functionalities

Beyond these core functionalities, some UTM solutions might offer

- **Data Loss Prevention (DLP):** DLP helps to prevent sensitive data from being exfiltrated from your network, whether intentionally or unintentionally.

- **Virtual Private Network (VPN) Management:** Certain UTM solutions include VPN management capabilities, making it easier to set up and manage secure remote access connections.

- **Sandboxing:** Sandboxing enables the safe detonation and analysis of suspicious files in a controlled environment, preventing them from infecting your network if they are malicious.

The specific functionalities provided by a UTM solution will differ depending on the vendor and model.

13.3.2 The Advantages of UTM Integration: A Unified Approach to Security

Implementing a UTM solution provides several benefits for organizations looking to strengthen their security posture:

- **Simplified Management:** A UTM solution combines multiple security tools on a single platform, streamlining security management and lowering administrative overhead. This frees up IT resources to work on more important tasks.

- **Enhanced Visibility:** UTM solutions provide a centralized view of your network's security, revealing valuable information about threats, vulnerabilities, and overall security posture. This comprehensive view allows you to make informed decisions about security strategies.

- **Improved Security Effectiveness:** UTM solutions provide a more comprehensive defense against cyber threats because they combine multiple security functionalities. This layered approach makes it harder for attackers to bypass your defense mechanisms.

- **Reduced Costs:** UTM solutions offer a more comprehensive defense against cyber threats by combining multiple security functionalities. This layered approach makes it more difficult for attackers to circumvent your defense mechanisms.

The reduced administrative burden leads to cost savings. However, it's important to remember that UTM solutions are not a silver bullet. Here are some factors to consider:

- **Complexity:** UTM solutions can be difficult to configure and manage, particularly for small businesses with limited IT resources.

- **Performance Impact:** UTMs have an impact on network performance, particularly when performing deep packet inspection or other resource-intensive tasks. Careful configuration and sizing of the UTM solution are critical to reducing performance degradation.

- **Scalability:** Ensure that the UTM solution you choose can scale to meet your organization's growing needs.

By carefully considering these factors and selecting a UTM solution that meets your specific needs, you can use its capabilities to establish a strong and efficient security posture for your organization.

CHAPTER 14

Cloud and Virtualization Security Considerations

As we navigate the ever-expanding digital landscape, protecting our data and resources becomes more important. The previous chapters taught you how to build strong network perimeter defenses and explore best practices for securing on-premises infrastructure. However, the digital landscape is constantly changing, and cloud computing and virtualization technologies are rapidly transforming how we store, access, and process information. This chapter delves into the security issues specific to these emerging environments. We'll look at ways to secure data in the cloud, reduce the risks associated with virtualization, and ensure a comprehensive security posture that includes both traditional and cloud-based infrastructure. Understanding these considerations and implementing appropriate security measures will allow you to confidently leverage the power and flexibility of cloud and virtualization technologies while ensuring the confidentiality, integrity, and availability of your valuable data.

© The Editor(s) (if applicable) and The Author(s), under exclusive license to APress Media, LLC, part of Springer Nature 2024
S. Lekkala and P. Gurijala, *Security and Privacy for Modern Networks*, https://doi.org/10.1007/979-8-8688-0823-4_14

14.1 Security Challenges in Cloud Computing Environments

Cloud computing has transformed how companies store, access, and process data. Its scalability, flexibility, and cost-effectiveness have led to widespread adoption among businesses of all sizes. However, migrating to the cloud introduces new security challenges that must be carefully considered.

14.1.1 Shared Responsibility Model: Understanding the Security Landscape

The shared responsibility model serves as the foundation for cloud security. In this model, the cloud service provider (CSP) is responsible for securing the underlying infrastructure, while the customer is still responsible for securing the data and applications stored on the cloud platform. This division of responsibilities necessitates a clear understanding of which security aspects are handled by the CSP and which require customer intervention.

- **Cloud Provider Responsibilities:** CSPs are in charge of ensuring the physical infrastructure, network security, and virtualization layer of their cloud platform. This includes securing data centers, enforcing access controls, and patching vulnerabilities in the cloud infrastructure.

- **Customer Responsibilities:** Customers are responsible for securing their data, applications, and access controls in the cloud. This includes tasks such as

  - Encrypting data at rest and in transit

- Managing user access and permissions

- Configuring security settings for cloud storage and services

- Implementing security best practices for cloud applications

A breakdown of these responsibilities encourages a collaborative approach to cloud security. By understanding their respective roles, the CSP and customer can collaborate to create a secure cloud environment.

14.1.2 Potential Security Risks: Navigating the Cloud Threat Landscape

Migrating to the cloud introduces potential security risks that organizations need to be aware of:

- **Data Breaches:** Cloud storage is a potential target for attackers looking to steal sensitive data. Encrypting data at rest and in transit is critical to mitigating this risk.

- **Insider Threats:** Malicious insiders with authorized access can be a major threat to cloud data security. Implementing strong access controls and monitoring user activity are critical security measures.

- **Shared Infrastructure Security Concerns:** Malicious insiders with authorized access pose a significant threat to cloud data security. Strong access controls and monitoring user activity are essential security precautions.

- **Account Hijacking:** Unauthorized access to a cloud account can give attackers control of sensitive data and resources. Enforcing multifactor authentication (MFA) for all cloud accounts significantly lowers this risk.

- **Misconfigurations:** Cloud environments provide a vast number of configuration options. Accidental misconfigurations can lead to security vulnerabilities. Understanding the best practices for cloud security configuration is critical.

Organizations can reduce their exposure to cloud-based threats by recognizing potential security risks and implementing appropriate safeguards.

14.1.3 Addressing Security Challenges: Strategies for a Secure Cloud Journey

Securing your cloud environment necessitates a proactive strategy that addresses the identified issues. Here are some key strategies to consider:

- **Data Security:** Implement strong data security measures, such as encryption of data at rest and in transit. Use cloud-based key management solutions to ensure encryption keys are securely stored and access is controlled.

- **Identity and Access Management (IAM):** Enforce robust identity and access management (IAM) practices. Use the need-to-know principle to grant users least privilege access. Implement multifactor authentication (MFA) to increase the security of all cloud account access.

- **Security Awareness and Training:** Educate your users about cloud security best practices. Teach them how to detect phishing attempts, avoid suspicious links, and report any security issues.

- **Security Monitoring:** Continuously monitor your cloud environment for any suspicious activity. Use cloud security monitoring tools to detect and respond to potential security incidents quickly.

- **Compliance Considerations:** Ensure that your cloud security posture complies with applicable industry regulations and compliance requirements. Several regulations require specific data security controls.

By implementing these strategies and maintaining a vigilant security posture, you can maximize the benefits of cloud computing while minimizing the security risks. Remember that cloud security is a shared responsibility. Collaborate effectively with your chosen CSP to ensure that your organization's cloud environment is secure and reliable.

14.2 Securing Virtual Network Functions (VNFs) and Services

Virtualization technologies have transformed IT infrastructure management by allowing organizations to consolidate resources, increase agility, and cut costs. The Virtual Network Function (VNF) is a core concept in network virtualization. VNFs are software applications that perform network functions previously provided by dedicated hardware appliances such as firewalls, load balancers, and intrusion detection systems (IDS). While virtualization provides numerous benefits, it also introduces new security concerns that must be carefully addressed.

14.2.1 Understanding the VNF Security Landscape: Potential Threats and Vulnerabilities

VNFs provide a flexible and scalable approach to network functions, but they are not without security concerns. Here are some key threats and vulnerabilities you should be aware of:

- **Supply Chain Attacks:** VNFs obtained from third-party vendors may introduce security vulnerabilities if their security practices are inadequate. Implementing measures to assess the security posture of VNF vendors is critical.

- **Misconfiguration Vulnerabilities:** VNFs must be properly configured to function securely. Misconfigurations can expose security vulnerabilities that attackers can exploit. Automating VNF deployments and ensuring consistent configurations can help to reduce this risk.

- **API Security Concerns:** VNFs frequently use APIs to communicate with other network components. Inadequate API security controls can leave VNFs vulnerable to unauthorized access and manipulation. Strong authentication and authorization mechanisms for VNF APIs are required.

- **Lateral Movement Risks:** Attackers who establish a foothold in a virtualized environment may use interconnected VNFs to move laterally across the network, potentially compromising other critical systems. Segmentation within the virtualized environment can help to limit the blast radius of an attack.

- **Denial-of-Service (DoS) Attacks:** VNFs, if not properly secured, can become targets for DoS attacks, disrupting network operations. This risk can be mitigated by implementing appropriate resource management and rate-limiting controls.

Understanding these potential threats and vulnerabilities allows organizations to take proactive steps to protect their VNF deployments.

14.2.2 Securing VNFs: A Multilayered Approach

Securing VNFs necessitates a multifaceted approach that addresses all known threats and vulnerabilities. Here are some critical security best practices to consider:

- **Vulnerability Management:** VNFs should be periodically scanned for vulnerabilities and patched as soon as possible. Patch management processes must be established to ensure that all VNF software components receive timely updates.

- **Microsegmentation:** Use microsegmentation in the virtualized environment to isolate VNFs and prevent lateral movement in the event of a security breach.

- **API Security:** Set up strong authentication and authorization controls for VNF APIs. Encrypt sensitive data transmitted via APIs.

- **Secure Boot and Secure VNF Lifecycle Management:** Implement secure boot mechanisms to ensure that only authorized software is executed on VNFs. Create a secure VNF lifecycle management process that covers VNF deployment, configuration, and decommissioning. Implement secure boot mechanisms to ensure that only authorized software is executed on VNFs. Create a secure VNF lifecycle management process that covers VNF deployment, configuration, and decommissioning.

- **Continuous Monitoring:** Continuously monitor VNF activity for unusual behavior. Use security information and event management (SIEM) solutions to correlate data from multiple sources and identify potential security incidents.

By following these best practices, organizations can create a more secure environment for VNF deployments, reducing the risks associated with virtualization and protecting the integrity of their network infrastructure.

14.2.3 The Future of VNF Security: Embracing Emerging Technologies

The landscape of VNF security is constantly evolving. Here are some emerging trends that hold promise for the future:

- **Containerization:** Containerization technologies offer a lightweight alternative to traditional virtualization and can potentially improve VNF security by isolating VNFs at a finer granularity.

- **Security Automation:** Constantly monitor VNF activity for any unusual behavior. Use security information and event management (SIEM) solutions to correlate events from various sources and identify potential security incidents.

- **Integration with Cloud Security Solutions:**
  Leveraging cloud security solutions provided by cloud
  providers can help to improve the security posture of
  VNFs deployed in cloud environments.

Organizations can ensure the long-term security of their VNF
deployments by staying informed about emerging trends and embracing
innovative security solutions as virtualization technologies advance.

14.3 Addressing Data Sovereignty and Cloud Privacy Concerns

Cloud computing provides numerous benefits, but it also raises concerns
about data sovereignty and privacy. Data sovereignty refers to the laws
and regulations that govern where and how data is stored and accessed or
transferred. Data privacy concerns center on how cloud service providers
(CSPs) manage and protect user data. Understanding these concerns and
implementing appropriate strategies are critical for organizations using the
cloud while maintaining compliance and user trust.

14.3.1 Understanding Data Sovereignty and Localization Regulations

Data sovereignty regulations vary by country and region. These regulations
dictate where data can be stored, processed, and accessed. Here's a
breakdown of key concepts:

- **Data Residency:** Data residency laws require that data
  be stored within a specific geographic location. This
  could be the country from which the data originated, or
  a specific region within that country.

- **Data Localization:** Data localization regulations extend beyond residency, limiting data transfers outside of the designated geographic location. This can present difficulties for organizations with global operations or those that require data transfer for processing or analytics purposes.

- **Data Accessibility by Law Enforcement:** Some regulations allow law enforcement agencies to access data stored within their jurisdiction, even if it belongs to a foreign entity. Understanding the legal implications is critical for organizations that operate in multiple countries.

Organizations migrating to the cloud must carefully consider data sovereignty regulations specific to their industry, as well as the location of their users' data.

14.3.2 Balancing Cloud Benefits with Data Privacy Concerns

Data privacy concerns are another important factor to consider when using cloud services. Here are some major areas of concern:

- **Data Security Practices of CSPs:** Organizations entrust CSPs with sensitive data. Understanding the CSP's data security policies, compliance certifications, and incident response procedures is critical.

- **Data Sharing with Third Parties:** Some CSPs may provide user data to third-party vendors for a variety of purposes. Organizations should scrutinize the CSP's data sharing practices to ensure they are consistent with their own data privacy policies.

- **User Control Over Data:** Organizations should ensure that users have control over their data in the cloud environment. This includes the ability to access, modify, and delete their data as needed.

Organizations can reduce the risks associated with cloud data storage by carefully evaluating these factors and selecting a reputable CSP with a proven track record of data privacy.

14.3.3 Strategies for Addressing Data Sovereignty and Privacy Concerns

Here are some key strategies for addressing data sovereignty and privacy concerns when using cloud services:

- **Conduct a Data Residency Assessment:** Determine the location of your data and the data residency rules that apply.

- **Choose a Compliant CSP:** Choose a CSP with a track record of adhering to relevant data sovereignty and privacy regulations.

- **Contractual Safeguards:** Negotiate clear contractual terms with your CSP regarding data residency, security practices, and user data ownership.

- **Data Encryption:** Encrypt sensitive data at rest and in transit to add an extra layer of protection.

- **Data Loss Prevention (DLP):** Implement DLP solutions to prevent unauthorized exfiltration of sensitive data from the cloud.

- **User Education:** Educate users on data privacy best practices and give them the ability to make informed decisions about their data in the cloud.

153

Implementing these strategies allows organizations to confidently use the cloud while adhering to data sovereignty regulations and protecting user privacy. Remember that data sovereignty and privacy are ongoing considerations. Maintaining a secure and compliant cloud environment requires staying up to date on evolving regulations and adapting your cloud strategy as needed.

CHAPTER 15

Endpoint and Mobile Security Imperatives

As we navigate the ever-expanding digital landscape, protecting our data at all touchpoints becomes critical. We've looked into ways to strengthen network perimeters, secure cloud environments, and reduce the risks associated with virtualization. However, our journey does not stop there. In today's mobile world, endpoints such as laptops, desktop computers, and mobile devices have become gateways to sensitive information and corporate resources. This chapter delves into the critical factors for endpoint and mobile security. We'll look at how to secure traditional desktops and laptops, mobile device management strategies, and emerging endpoint security threats such as ransomware and zero-day attacks. By understanding these factors and implementing strong endpoint security measures, you can build a comprehensive defense that protects your valuable data wherever it goes.

15.1 Strategies for Securing Network Endpoints

Laptops, desktop computers, and mobile devices are now commonplace in the digital world. They are the primary tools employees use to access corporate resources, connect to networks, and process sensitive data.

© The Editor(s) (if applicable) and The Author(s), under exclusive license to APress Media, LLC, part of Springer Nature 2024
S. Lekkala and P. Gurijala, *Security and Privacy for Modern Networks*,
https://doi.org/10.1007/979-8-8688-0823-4_15

However, this widespread use also introduces significant security challenges. Endpoints represent potential entry points for cyberattacks, and a compromised endpoint can expose your entire network to a multitude of threats. This chapter equips you with the knowledge to fortify your defense mechanisms and implement robust endpoint security measures.

15.1.1 Understanding the Endpoint Security Landscape

The endpoint security landscape encompasses various aspects:

- **Operating System Security:** Securing the operating system on endpoints is critical. This includes updating operating systems with the most recent security patches, enforcing strong password policies, and disabling unnecessary services.

- **Application Security:** Many endpoint vulnerabilities result from out-of-date or insecure applications. Enforce a policy of only using authorized applications and keeping them up to date with the latest security fixes.

- **Endpoint Detection and Response (EDR) Solutions:** EDR solutions continuously monitor endpoints for suspicious activity, allowing for real-time threat detection and quick response to security incidents.

- **User Education and Awareness:** It is critical to educate users on best practices for cybersecurity. Educate them on how to recognize phishing attempts, avoid unsafe browsing habits, and report suspicious activity.

Understanding these key elements enables you to create a comprehensive endpoint security strategy that addresses vulnerabilities throughout the endpoint ecosystem. Understanding these key elements enables you to create a comprehensive endpoint security strategy that addresses vulnerabilities throughout the endpoint ecosystem.

15.1.2 Securing Traditional Desktops and Laptops

Traditional desktops and laptops are still widely used in today's workplaces. Here are key strategies for securing them:

- **Operating System Updates:** Ensure that operating systems are promptly updated to address known vulnerabilities. Configure automatic updates whenever possible to make this process easier.

- **Strong Password Policies:** Enforce strong password policies that include minimum password length, complexity requirements, and regular password changes. Multifactor authentication (MFA) provides an additional level of security.

- **Application Whitelisting:** Consider implementing application whitelisting to prevent users from running unauthorized applications on their devices.

- **Endpoint Protection Software:** Deploy endpoint protection software to protect against malware, viruses, and other threats in real time. These solutions typically include features like anti-malware scanning, intrusion prevention, and application management.

- **Physical Security:** Implement physical security measures to protect the devices. These could include requiring strong passwords on login screens, encrypting data at rest, and utilizing device encryption features.

Implementing these practices will significantly reduce the risk of compromise for traditional desktop and laptop endpoints.

15.1.3 Mobile Device Management (MDM) for a Secure Mobile Workforce

The proliferation of mobile devices, such as smartphones and tablets, necessitates effective mobile device management (MDM) strategies. MDM solutions provide centralized control over mobile devices connected to your network.

- **Device Enrollment and Configuration:** MDM enables you to enforce enrollment policies that limit which devices can connect to your network and configure security settings on enrolled devices.

- **Application Management:** MDM solutions allow you to manage mobile applications, such as distributing approved apps, limiting unauthorized apps, and remotely wiping data from lost or stolen devices.

- **Data Security:** MDM can enforce data encryption on mobile devices to protect sensitive data both at rest and in transit.

- **Remote Wipe Capability:** In the event of a lost or stolen device, MDM enables you to remotely wipe it, preventing unauthorized access to corporate data.

Implementing an MDM solution and enforcing appropriate mobile security policies will allow you to expand your security posture to include your organization's growing mobile device landscape.

15.2 Addressing the Unique Security Needs of Mobile Devices

While mobile device management (MDM) provides a solid foundation for securing mobile devices, they pose unique security challenges that necessitate additional considerations. Unlike traditional desktop computers, which are fixed to a specific location, mobile devices are inherently portable and frequently connect to multiple networks. This mobility introduces several security risks, necessitating a multilayered defense strategy.

15.2.1 BYOD (Bring Your Own Device) Security Considerations

The Bring Your Own Device (BYOD) trend enables employees to use their personal devices for work. While BYOD provides flexibility and convenience, it raises security concerns:

- **Increased Attack Surface:** A wider range of device types and operating systems broadens the attack surface. Maintaining consistent security configurations across a diverse device landscape can be difficult.

- **Data Leakage:** Accidental or malicious data leakage from personal devices is a serious threat. To mitigate this risk, implement data loss prevention (DLP) solutions and educate users on proper data handling practices.

- **Limited Control:** Organizations have less control over the security posture of personal devices than company-issued devices. MDM can help bridge some of the gap, but it is critical to establish clear policies and user agreements regarding BYOD practices.

BYOD programs require careful risk assessment and the implementation of strong security measures.

15.2.2 Securing Mobile Devices Against Emerging Threats

Mobile devices are prime targets for emerging cyber threats:

- **Phishing Attacks:** Phishing attempts aimed at stealing user credentials or tricking them into downloading malware are common on mobile devices. Educating users on how to recognize phishing tactics and implementing email security measures that filter malicious messages can significantly reduce the risk.

- **Malicious Applications:** Third-party app stores may contain malicious applications. Enforce MDM policies that limit app downloads to approved app stores, and use mobile antivirus solutions to detect and prevent malware on devices.

- **Unsecured Public Wi-Fi:** Eavesdropping and man-in-the-middle attacks thrive on public Wi-Fi networks, which are frequently unsecured. Discourage users from accessing sensitive information over public Wi-Fi, and consider using Virtual Private Network (VPN) solutions to encrypt data traffic on mobile devices.

- **Social Engineering Attacks:** Social engineering techniques can be adapted for mobile devices. Educate users on how to spot and avoid social engineering scams that try to trick them into disclosing sensitive information or clicking on malicious links.

Understanding these emerging threats and implementing appropriate safeguards can help you reduce the risk of mobile device compromise while also protecting your organization's data.

15.2.3 Device Encryption for Comprehensive Mobile Data Protection

Data encryption is essential for protecting mobile devices. Here's why:

- **Lost or Stolen Devices:** In the event that your device is lost or stolen, encryption protects your data from unauthorized access. Even if attackers take physical possession of the device, they will be unable to decrypt the data without the encryption key.

- **Data at Rest:** Encryption protects information stored on the device itself. This includes data stored on both internal storage and removable storage cards.

- **Data in Transit:** Data encryption protects information as it travels between the mobile device and other systems. This is especially important when accessing public Wi-Fi networks.

Implementing full-disk encryption on mobile devices can significantly reduce the risk of data breaches while also protecting the confidentiality of your sensitive information.

By recognizing mobile devices' unique security requirements and implementing a comprehensive security strategy that includes MDM, user education, and robust data protection measures, you can empower your mobile workforce while protecting your organization's data.

15.3 Implementing EDR Systems for Endpoint Threat Response

Traditional antivirus software is critical for endpoint security, but it is no longer sufficient to combat today's sophisticated cyber threats. Endpoint Detection and Response (EDR) systems take a more advanced approach, continuously monitoring endpoints for suspicious activity and allowing for faster response to security incidents.

15.3.1 EDR: Beyond Antivirus – Proactive Threat Detection and Response

EDR systems go beyond the signature-based detection methods used in traditional antivirus solutions. Here's how EDR provides a more comprehensive approach:

- **Advanced Malware Detection:** EDR systems use advanced behavioral analytics to detect anomalous activity that could indicate malware infection, even if the type of malware is unknown (zero-day threats).

- **Endpoint Visibility and Context:** EDR solutions provide detailed visibility into endpoint activity by collecting and analyzing a broader range of data than traditional antivirus software. This enables a more comprehensive understanding of potential threats and the context in which they arise.

- **Incident Investigation and Threat Hunting:** EDR enables forensic analysis of security incidents, allowing security teams to investigate the root cause of an attack and determine the scope of the breach. EDR also enables proactive threat hunting, allowing security teams to look for indicators of compromise (IOCs) even before an attack occurs.

- **Automated Threat Response:** Some EDR solutions include automated incident response capabilities. These can automate tasks such as isolating infected endpoints, quarantining suspicious files, and starting remediation procedures.

EDR is a significant advancement in endpoint security, allowing for faster and more effective detection, investigation, and response to threats.

15.3.2 Selecting and Implementing an EDR Solution

Choosing and implementing an EDR solution requires careful consideration.

- **EDR Feature Set:** Evaluate the specific EDR features provided by various vendors. Ensure that the solution meets your organization's needs and threat profile.

- **Integration with Existing Security Tools:** Consider how the EDR solution integrates with your existing security infrastructure, including firewalls, intrusion detection/prevention systems (IDS/IPS), and security information and event management (SIEM) tools.

- **Deployment and Management:** Evaluate the specific EDR features provided by various vendors. Ensure that the solution meets your organization's needs and threat profile.

- **EDR Expertise:** Implementing and deploying an EDR solution effectively frequently necessitates specialized knowledge. Evaluate your organization's in-house security expertise or look into managed EDR services offered by security providers.

By carefully considering these factors, you can choose an EDR solution that significantly improves your endpoint security posture.

15.3.3 Leveraging EDR for a Proactive Security Defense

EDR enables security teams to shift from reactive to proactive security postures. Here's how:

- **Improved Threat Detection:** EDR's advanced capabilities allow for early detection of threats, potentially before they cause significant damage.

- **Faster Incident Response:** EDR enables rapid response to security incidents, reducing the window of opportunity for attackers.

- **Enhanced Threat Intelligence:** EDR solutions collect valuable information about endpoint activity and threats encountered. This information can be used to strengthen your overall security posture and guide future threat hunting efforts.

- **Reduced Security Costs:** EDR can help reduce the financial impact of security incidents by allowing for earlier detection and response to threats.

Implementing and integrating an EDR solution into your overall security strategy can provide you with a significant advantage in the ongoing battle against cyber threats. EDR provides you with the tools you need to proactively identify and respond to threats before they compromise your sensitive data and disrupt your operations.

CHAPTER 16

Leveraging AI and Machine Learning for Cyber Defense

This chapter delves into the fascinating world of artificial intelligence (AI) and machine learning (ML) in cybersecurity. We will look at how these powerful technologies are transforming threat detection, incident response, and overall security posture. From automating routine tasks to identifying hidden patterns in complex data, AI and machine learning are becoming indispensable tools in the fight against cybercrime. This chapter will help you understand how AI and ML are transforming cybersecurity and how you can use them to strengthen your organization's defense mechanisms.

16.1 Applying AI to Enhance Threat Detection Capabilities

In recent years, the threat landscape has grown increasingly complex and sophisticated. Cyber attackers utilize advanced multi-vector attacks that can bypass traditional security controls. As a result of these advances, cyber crime continues to rise at an alarming rate. To combat these

© The Editor(s) (if applicable) and The Author(s), under exclusive license to APress Media, LLC, part of Springer Nature 2024
S. Lekkala and P. Gurijala, *Security and Privacy for Modern Networks*, https://doi.org/10.1007/979-8-8688-0823-4_16

attacks, organizations require new capabilities to augment their cyber defense. This has driven the necessity for artificial intelligence (AI) and machine learning (ML) technologies to be incorporated in cyber defense mechanisms. AI and ML provide an effective new approach to combating this growing threat. Organizations that use AI and ML can significantly improve their threat detection capabilities and proactively defend against cyberattacks.

16.1.1 The Power of AI and ML in Threat Detection

AI and ML offer unique capabilities that can be harnessed to improve threat detection:

- **Advanced Anomaly Detection:** AI and machine learning algorithms can analyze large amounts of security data, such as network traffic logs, endpoint activity, user behavior, and system logs. These algorithms can detect unusual patterns and deviations from normal behavior, which may indicate a potential security incident. This advanced anomaly detection allows for the identification of previously unknown zero-day threats.

- **Automated Threat Hunting:** Security analysts are frequently overwhelmed by the sheer volume of security data. AI and machine learning can automate threat hunting tasks, allowing security personnel to focus on investigation and response. ML algorithms can continuously scan for indicators of compromise (IOCs) and suspicious activity, significantly reducing the time required to detect potential threats.

- **Improved Threat Analysis and Prioritization:** AI and ML can examine security data to determine the severity and potential impact of a detected threat. This enables security teams to prioritize their response efforts and concentrate on the most pressing threats first.

- **Continuous Learning and Adaptation:** AI and ML models are always learning and evolving. As they process more data and encounter new threats, they improve their ability to detect and classify potential security incidents.

By incorporating AI and ML into your security infrastructure, you can significantly improve threat detection. These technologies can help you identify threats more quickly and accurately, freeing up valuable security resources for more important tasks.

16.1.2 Challenges and Considerations for AI-Powered Threat Detection

While AI and ML have tremendous potential, there are some challenges to consider:

- **Data Quality:** The quality of the data used to train AI and ML models has a significant impact on their effectiveness. Inaccurate or incomplete data can result in false positives and missed detections.

- **Explainability and Transparency:** AI models can sometimes produce results without providing a clear explanation for how they arrived at a specific conclusion. This lack of transparency can make it difficult to understand why a threat was identified, impeding the investigation process.

- **Security Expertise:** Using AI and ML for threat detection frequently necessitates specialized knowledge to configure, manage, and interpret the results produced by these models.

Despite these challenges, AI and machine learning are rapidly evolving, and threat detection capabilities are constantly improving. Organizations can use these technologies to create a more robust and proactive security posture by understanding their potential as well as their limitations.

16.2 Machine Learning Techniques for Security Data Analysis

As we discussed in the previous section, artificial intelligence (AI) and machine learning (ML) are transforming the field of cybersecurity. This section delves deeper into specific machine learning techniques that are especially beneficial for security data analysis. By understanding these techniques, you can gain a practical understanding of how AI and ML can be applied to strengthen your organization's defenses.

16.2.1 Classification Algorithms for Threat Detection

Classification algorithms are a key machine learning technique for threat detection. These algorithms analyze data and assign it to predefined categories. In security contexts, classification algorithms can be trained to detect malicious activity in network traffic, user behavior, and system logs.

- **Supervised Learning:** Supervised learning algorithms require labeled data sets to train. Security analysts classify data samples as malicious or benign.

The algorithm learns from these labeled examples and creates a model that can be used to classify new, previously unseen data. Support Vector Machines (SVMs) and Random Forests are two commonly used supervised learning algorithms for threat detection.

- **Unsupervised Learning:** Unsupervised learning algorithms work on unlabeled data. They can be used to detect patterns and anomalies in security data that differ from the expected baseline. This can be useful for detecting zero-day threats or other novel attacks that have not been seen before. Anomaly detection algorithms such as K-means clustering and Local Outlier Factor (LOF) are useful for unsupervised learning in security data analysis.

16.2.2 Machine Learning for User and Entity Behavior Analytics (UEBA)

User and Entity Behavior Analytics (UEBA) uses machine learning to analyze user and entity activity within a system. UEBA systems track activity patterns and detect anomalies that could indicate compromised accounts, insider threats, or other security incidents.

- **Building User Baselines:** UEBA systems calculate baselines for typical user behavior by examining factors such as login times, data access patterns, and device usage.

- **Detecting Anomalous Activity:** Machine learning algorithms continuously monitor user and entity activity, identifying deviations from established baselines that may indicate potential security risks.

- **Investigating and Responding to Threats:** UEBA systems can provide valuable insights to security analysts looking into potential threats discovered through anomalous activity detection.

Organizations that implement UEBA solutions powered by machine learning can gain a better understanding of user and entity behavior within their systems, allowing them to proactively identify and mitigate insider threats and account compromise attempts.

16.2.3 The Future of Machine Learning in Security Data Analysis

Machine learning is a rapidly evolving field, with new applications in security data analysis emerging all the time. Here's a look at what the future holds:

- **Improved Threat Detection Accuracy:** As machine learning models are exposed to more data and continuously refined, their threat detection accuracy will improve.

- **Automated Incident Response:** Machine learning could play a larger role in automating incident response tasks like isolating compromised systems and removing threats.

- **Integration with Security Automation Platforms:** Machine learning is likely to become more closely integrated with Security Automation Platforms (SOAR) in order to streamline security operations and orchestrate automated responses to incidents.

Organizations can create a more robust and adaptive security posture in the ever-changing threat landscape by staying up to date on advances in machine learning and its security applications.

16.3 Ethical Implications and Best Practices for AI in Security

Artificial intelligence (AI) has enormous potential for improving security, but its use raises ethical concerns that must be carefully addressed. AI in security applications must be developed and deployed responsibly, just like any other powerful technology.

16.3.1 Bias and Fairness in AI Algorithms

The possibility of bias is a major ethical concern with AI. AI algorithms are trained on data sets created by humans, which may inadvertently encode human biases. When applied to security contexts, biased AI models may result in unfair profiling, uneven application of security measures, or even discrimination.

- **Mitigating Bias:** Organizations can reduce bias by carefully selecting and curating training data sets for AI models used in cybersecurity. Furthermore, using fairness metrics and algorithms designed to detect and address bias can help ensure more equitable and ethical AI-powered security solutions.

16.3.2 Transparency and Explainability of AI Decisions

Another ethical consideration is the lack of transparency in certain AI models. These models can occasionally produce results without providing a clear explanation for their reasoning. In security contexts, a lack of transparency can make it difficult to understand why a specific individual or activity was marked as suspicious.

- **Explainable AI (XAI):** The field of Explainable AI (XAI) is actively developing techniques for making AI models more transparent and understandable. Understanding the reasoning behind an AI's decision enables security analysts to make more informed decisions and ensure the responsible use of AI-powered security tools.

16.3.3 Accountability for AI-Driven Security Decisions

When AI is used to make security decisions, the question of accountability arises. Who is responsible if an AI system makes a mistake or misidentifies an innocent person as a threat? Is it the AI model developers, the organization that is deploying the technology, or the AI system itself?

- **Establishing Clear Lines of Accountability:** Organizations that use AI in security should establish clear lines of accountability for the decisions made by their systems. This includes having human oversight mechanisms in place to review AI outputs and ensure the technology is used responsibly.

16.3.4 Privacy Concerns and Data Security

Security AI applications frequently rely on the analysis of large amounts of data, such as user activity, network traffic, and other potentially sensitive information. It is critical to protect the privacy of this information and implement strong security measures to prevent unauthorized access or misuse.

- **Data Minimization and User Consent:** Organizations should strive to limit the amount of data collected for AI-powered security solutions and obtain explicit user consent before collecting and using such data. Furthermore, implementing strong data security practices is critical for protecting sensitive information throughout the AI lifecycle.

16.3.5 Human-in-the-Loop Security with AI

AI is a powerful tool, but it should not be used to completely replace human judgment. Security decisions, especially those with significant consequences, should be made with a human in the loop. AI can be used to detect and analyze threats, but human security professionals should make the final decisions and take the necessary actions.

By acknowledging these ethical considerations and following best practices for responsible AI development and deployment, organizations can harness the power of AI in security while mitigating potential risks and ensuring ethical use of this transformative technology.

16.4 Importance of User Awareness Training in Conjunction with AI-Powered Security Solutions

Despite advances in security technologies such as artificial intelligence (AI) and machine learning (ML), human awareness remains a critical line of defense against cyber threats. AI-powered security solutions are effective tools, but they cannot completely eliminate the risks associated with social engineering attacks, phishing attempts, and other human-targeted tactics. This is where user awareness training comes in. By educating users about cybersecurity best practices and empowering them to identify and avoid security risks, organizations can significantly strengthen their overall security posture.

16.4.1 Why User Awareness Training Is Crucial in the Age of AI Security

While AI is excellent at analyzing large amounts of data and identifying patterns, it cannot replace human judgment and critical thinking abilities. Here's why user awareness training is still essential:

- **Social Engineering Attacks:** Social engineering tactics exploit human emotions to trick users into disclosing sensitive information or clicking on malicious links. AI cannot effectively defend against these attacks, which frequently bypass technical security controls. Users who are educated about social engineering red flags are better able to identify and resist such attempts.

- **Phishing Awareness:** Phishing emails are a common threat, as they are often designed to appear legitimate and trick users into clicking on malicious links or attachments. Training users to recognize phishing tactics, such as suspicious sender addresses, urgency prompts, and grammatical errors, reduces the likelihood of successful phishing attacks.

- **Strong Password Habits:** Weak passwords are a significant security risk. Educating users on how to create strong passwords, enforcing password complexity requirements, and implementing multifactor authentication (MFA) greatly reduces the risk of unauthorized account access.

- **Data Security Best Practices:** Employees can benefit from user awareness training, which can teach them data security best practices such as being cautious about what information they communicate online, avoiding public Wi-Fi for sensitive activities, and reporting suspicious activity to information security teams.

Understanding these key areas allows organizations to design user awareness training programs that address the changing threat landscape and empower users to take an active role in their organization's security posture.

16.4.2 Benefits of Combining AI Security with User Education

The combination of AI-powered security solutions and user awareness training provides a comprehensive approach to cybersecurity.

- **Enhanced Threat Detection and Response:** AI can continuously monitor network activity and user behavior, detecting anomalies that may indicate a threat. Users who are concerned about security can report suspicious activity or emails to security teams, which will help to improve threat detection and response capabilities.

- **Reduced Risk of Human Error:** Human error can sometimes be the cause of data breaches or security incidents. User awareness training can help to reduce these risks by educating users about proper security protocols and best practices.

- **Stronger Security Culture:** A combination of AI-powered security and user awareness training helps to foster a security-conscious culture within an organization. Employees become more committed to protecting sensitive data and are more likely to report suspicious activity.

177

Organizations can create a layered defense by combining AI power with a well-trained and security-conscious workforce.

16.4.3 Developing Effective User Awareness Training Programs

Here are some important considerations for developing effective user awareness training programs:

- **Tailored Training Content:** Training materials should be tailored to the specific needs and roles of each user group within the organization. Technical users may require more in-depth training on security best practices, whereas non-technical users may benefit from broader awareness training aimed at detecting phishing attempts and social engineering techniques.

- **Regular Training and Updates:** Cybersecurity threats are constantly evolving, so regular user awareness training is required. Refresher courses and updates on new threats and attack vectors keep users informed and alert.

- **Engaging Training Methods:** Cybersecurity threats are constantly evolving, so regular user awareness training is required. Refresher courses and updates on new threats and attack vectors keep users informed and alert.

- **Measuring Training Effectiveness:** It is critical to evaluate the effectiveness of user awareness training programs. This can be accomplished through phishing simulations, knowledge assessment tests, or surveys that assess user comprehension and retention of key security concepts.

Organizations can empower their users to become valuable assets in the fight against cybercrime by implementing a comprehensive user awareness training program alongside AI-powered security solutions. Remember that cybersecurity is a shared responsibility. Organizations can build a strong security posture that protects sensitive data and defends against evolving cyber threats by combining advanced technology and human awareness.

CHAPTER 17

Case Studies

The theoretical foundations explored in this book will prepare you to design and implement effective security strategies. The true test, however, will be to apply this knowledge in real-world scenarios. This chapter delves into case studies demonstrating how organizations have implemented the various security measures discussed throughout the book. Examining these successes and failures will provide you with valuable insights into the practical application of security principles, as well as the importance of tailoring solutions to specific situations.

17.1 Target Breach: A Case Study in Network Segmentation and Perimeter Defense Failures

The 2013 Target data breach remains a watershed moment in cybersecurity history, exposing millions of customers' personal information and highlighting critical security flaws. This case study delves into the specifics of the breach, emphasizing the role of network segmentation (Chapter 8) and strong perimeter defense mechanisms (Chapter 12) in preventing such large-scale attacks.

© The Editor(s) (if applicable) and The Author(s), under exclusive license to APress Media, LLC, part of Springer Nature 2024
S. Lekkala and P. Gurijala, *Security and Privacy for Modern Networks*, https://doi.org/10.1007/979-8-8688-0823-4_17

Incident Overview

In December 2013, Target suffered a massive data breach that exposed the payment information of over 40 million customers. Hackers gained access to Target's network via a seemingly innocuous entry point: a third-party vendor's HVAC system. They exploited a flaw in the vendor's network security, eventually gaining access to Target's internal network. Once inside, they were able to move laterally across the network due to inadequate segmentation, eventually reaching and compromising point-of-sale (POS) systems that stored customer payment information.

Security Failures

This breach revealed critical vulnerabilities in Target's security posture, particularly in two key areas:

1. **Network Segmentation (Chapter 8):** Network segmentation is the division of a network into smaller, isolated segments. This keeps unauthorized access in one segment from jeopardizing critical systems and data in another. The target's network lacked proper segmentation, allowing attackers to move freely once they gained initial access.

2. **Perimeter Defense (Chapter 12):** Perimeter defense mechanisms are the primary line of defense against external attacks. They usually include firewalls, intrusion detection systems (IDS), and intrusion prevention systems (IPS). Target most likely had some perimeter defense in place, but they were either ineffective or misconfigured, allowing the attackers to bypass them and infiltrate the network.

Consequences of the Breach

The Target breach caused significant financial losses for the company, including fines, legal settlements, and customer compensation. Furthermore, it harmed Target's reputation and undermined customer trust.

Lessons Learned

The Target breach serves as a stark reminder of the value of a multilayered security strategy. Here are the key takeaways:

- **Network Segmentation:** Implement network segmentation to keep critical systems and data separate from less secure segments. This reduces the potential damage resulting from a successful breach.

- **Perimeter Defense:** Enhance perimeter defense with strong firewalls, IDS/IPS systems, and regular security assessments to detect and address vulnerabilities.

- **Third-Party Risk Management:** Extend security procedures to third-party vendors. Ensure that vendors have adequate security measures in place to keep them from becoming a vulnerability.

- **Regular Security Audits:** Conduct regular security audits to identify and address potential vulnerabilities in your network's security posture.

Learning from the Target breach allows organizations to take proactive steps to strengthen their security posture and reduce the risk of future attacks. Organizations can improve the security of their data and customers by implementing effective network segmentation and robust perimeter defenses.

17.2 Maersk Ransomware Attack: A Case Study in Endpoint Security and Intrusion Detection

The 2017 Maersk ransomware attack crippled operations at a global shipping conglomerate, emphasizing the importance of endpoint security (Chapter 15) and intrusion detection and response (Chapter 10) systems in today's threat environment. This case study delves into the specifics of the attack and the security flaws that enabled it to wreak havoc on Maersk's global network.

Incident Overview

In June 2017, Maersk was hit by a NotPetya ransomware attack. This sophisticated malware quickly spread throughout the company's network, encrypting critical data and disrupting operations at ports worldwide. The attack resulted in significant financial losses for Maersk, which hampered shipping operations and delayed cargo deliveries.

Security Weaknesses

The Maersk attack revealed vulnerabilities in two critical areas of Maersk's security posture:

1. **Endpoint Security (Chapter 15):** Endpoint security refers to the tools and techniques used to safeguard individual devices such as desktop computers, laptops, and servers. This typically includes antivirus software, endpoint detection and response (EDR) systems, and proper patching protocols. While Maersk most likely had some endpoint security measures in place, they could have been ineffective or outdated, allowing the ransomware to infect a large number of devices on the network.

2. **Intrusion Detection and Response (Chapter 10):**
   Intrusion detection and response (IDS/IPS) systems
   scan network traffic for unusual activity and can take
   automated action to mitigate threats. An effective
   IDS/IPS system could have detected the initial
   infection attempt and stopped the ransomware from
   spreading across the network.

Impact of the Attack

The Maersk ransomware attack caused significant disruptions in global shipping operations. Terminals were closed, cargo deliveries were delayed, and the company experienced significant financial losses. The attack also harmed Maersk's reputation while highlighting the vulnerability of critical infrastructure to cyberattacks.

Lessons Learned

The Maersk attack is a chilling reminder of the devastating consequences of ransomware attacks. Here are the key takeaways:

- **Endpoint Security:** Implement strong endpoint security solutions, such as antivirus software, EDR systems, and regular application patches. These tools can help prevent malware infections and restrict the spread of ransomware.

- **Intrusion Detection and Response:** Set up and maintain effective IDS/IPS systems to monitor network traffic for suspicious activity. These systems can provide early warning of potential attacks, allowing for a more rapid response.

- **Incident Response Planning:** Create a comprehensive incident response plan outlining procedures for detecting, mitigating, and recovering from cyberattacks. This plan should include steps for restoring data, reducing downtime, and effectively communicating with stakeholders.

- **Employee Training:** Educate employees on cybersecurity best practices, such as recognizing phishing attempts and avoiding suspicious links and attachments. A security-conscious workforce can serve as the first line of defense against cyberattacks.

Organizations can learn from the Maersk attack and prioritize endpoint security while implementing robust intrusion detection and response systems. These safeguards can significantly improve an organization's ability to defend against ransomware attacks and mitigate potential damage.

17.3 Equifax Data Breach: A Case Study in Human Error and Perimeter Defense Failures

The 2017 Equifax data breach exposed nearly 150 million Americans' sensitive information, emphasizing the importance of human awareness training (Chapter 5) and strong perimeter defense (Chapter 13) in safeguarding sensitive data. This case study delves into the specifics of the breach, examining the security flaws that allowed hackers to access a massive amount of personal information.

Incident Overview

In July 2017, Equifax, a major credit reporting agency, experienced a data breach that compromised millions of Americans' Social Security numbers, birthdates, and home addresses. Hackers exploited a vulnerability in a publicly accessible web application, emphasizing the importance of both user awareness training and timely security updates.

Security Failures

The Equifax breach points to two key security failures:

1. **Human Error and User Awareness (Chapter 5):** The attackers gained initial access by exploiting a previously known vulnerability in a web application server. This vulnerability had a patch available, but it appears Equifax failed to install it in a timely fashion. This lapse in patching procedures could be attributed to a lack of user awareness training for IT staff regarding the importance of applying security updates on time.

2. **Perimeter Defense (Chapter 13):** Equifax's perimeter defense, including firewalls and intrusion detection systems (IDS), may have been insufficient or misconfigured. This enabled the attackers to remain undetected on the network for an extended period of time, giving them access to sensitive databases containing consumer information.

Consequences of the Breach

The Equifax breach led to a significant loss of trust in the credit reporting agency. Equifax faced regulatory penalties, lawsuits, and reputational harm. Millions of consumers were at risk of identity theft and fraud.

Lessons Learned

The Equifax breach serves as a cautionary tale about the human factor in cybersecurity. Here are the key takeaways:

- **User Awareness Training:** Implement regular user awareness training programs for all employees, particularly IT professionals. These programs should teach employees how to recognize phishing attempts, the value of strong passwords, and the critical role of timely security updates.

- **Patch Management:** Develop and enforce strict patch management procedures to ensure that all systems and software receive security updates on time.

- **Perimeter Security:** Regularly evaluate and strengthen perimeter defense, such as firewalls and IDS/IPS systems. These systems should be configured to detect and prevent suspicious network activity.

- **Data Security Best Practices:** Implement strong data security best practices, such as encryption and access controls, to reduce the potential impact of a data breach.

Organizations can learn from the Equifax breach to prioritize user awareness training and implement effective patch management procedures. Furthermore, strengthening perimeter defense and following data security best practices can significantly reduce the risk of similar attacks while safeguarding sensitive consumer information.

CHAPTER 18

Preparing for Future Technological Shifts

The cybersecurity landscape is constantly changing, thanks to technological advancements and attackers' ingenuity. While the fundamental principles of security remain constant, new technologies pose unique challenges that necessitate innovative security solutions. This chapter delves into some of the upcoming technological shifts and their potential impact on cybersecurity. Organizations can maintain a strong security posture against emerging threats by proactively preparing for these changes.

18.1 Understanding IoT Security Challenges and Solutions

The Internet of Things (IoT) is a vast and ever-expanding network of Internet-connected devices ranging from personal appliances to industrial control systems. While these devices provide convenience and automation, they also raise serious security concerns. This section delves into the specific security concerns associated with IoT devices and discusses potential solutions to mitigate these risks.

© The Editor(s) (if applicable) and The Author(s), under exclusive license to APress Media, LLC, part of Springer Nature 2024
S. Lekkala and P. Gurijala, *Security and Privacy for Modern Networks*,
https://doi.org/10.1007/979-8-8688-0823-4_18

- **Challenge – Expanding Attack Surface:** The sheer number and variety of IoT devices creates a massive and expanding attack surface for malicious actors. These devices frequently have limited processing power and weak security measures, leaving them vulnerable to botnets, malware, and other cyberattacks.

- **Security Considerations**

  - **Secure Development and Deployment:** Manufacturers of IoT devices must prioritize security throughout the development process. This includes secure coding practices, robust authentication mechanisms, and ensuring that deployed devices receive regular security updates.

  - **Network Segmentation:** Isolating IoT devices from critical systems and data can help to mitigate the potential damage caused by a compromised device. Network segmentation provides a layered defense, preventing attackers who gain access to an IoT device from easily accessing sensitive data on other parts of the network.

  - **Vulnerability Management:** Organizations should regularly scan IoT devices for vulnerabilities and apply patches as soon as they are possible. This includes staying informed about known vulnerabilities and promptly applying security updates from device manufacturers.

Organizations and manufacturers can improve the security of IoT devices by implementing these security considerations. A comprehensive approach that combines secure development practices, network segmentation, and proactive vulnerability management is required to mitigate the security risks associated with the growing IoT landscape.

18.2 Anticipating the Security Impact of Quantum Computing

The emergence of quantum computing poses a significant challenge to the current cybersecurity paradigm. Traditional encryption methods are based on complex mathematical problems that are difficult to solve with current computing power. These methods are the foundation of secure communication and data protection in a variety of industries, from financial transactions to national security.

18.2.1 The Threat Posed by Quantum Computers

Quantum computers use quantum mechanics principles to perform calculations that are fundamentally different from those performed by traditional computers. This enables them to solve certain problems exponentially faster, such as those underlying many widely used encryption algorithms. Simply put, a powerful enough quantum computer could potentially break the encryption that protects sensitive information, making it vulnerable to unauthorized access.

18.2.2 Potential Consequences of Broken Encryption

The successful decryption of currently encrypted data may have a devastating impact on various aspects of our digital world:

- **Compromised Financial Transactions:** Financial institutions rely heavily on encryption to safeguard sensitive financial data like credit card numbers and account information. If quantum computers can break current encryption methods, it could result in widespread financial fraud and identity theft.

- **Erosion of National Security:** Governments and militaries use strong encryption to protect sensitive information and communication channels. The ability to decrypt current encryption could jeopardize sensitive national security information and disrupt critical military operations.

- **Loss of Privacy:** Encryption is widely used to protect personal data, including online communications and medical records. If current encryption methods are found to be vulnerable, it could result in widespread privacy breaches and the exposure of sensitive personal information.

18.2.3 The Race for Post-Quantum Cryptography

Recognizing the potential threat posed by quantum computers, cryptographers are working to develop Post-Quantum Cryptography (PQC) algorithms. These new algorithms are intended to be resistant to attacks by quantum computers and to provide a more secure foundation for data encryption in the quantum age.

The development and adoption of PQC standards is a continuous process. Organizations can, however, prepare for the eventual transition to new encryption methods by taking the following steps:

- **Staying Informed About PQC Developments:** Monitor advances in PQC research and stay current on the standardization process.

- **Evaluating PQC Compatibility:** Determine the compatibility of current systems and infrastructure with potential PQC algorithms.

- **Developing a Migration Strategy:** Formulate a plan for transitioning to PQC algorithms when mature standards become available.

Organizations can ensure the long-term security of their data and critical infrastructure by proactively preparing for the potential impact of quantum computing.

18.3 Preparing for Breakthroughs in Encryption and Cyber Defense

The relentless pursuit of robust cybersecurity necessitates ongoing innovation in encryption and defensive techniques. While advances in encryption aim to keep up with evolving threats, breakthroughs in cyber defense can significantly improve an organization's ability to detect and respond to attacks. This section looks at some of the anticipated breakthroughs in these areas and how they might affect the future of cybersecurity.

18.3.1 The Promise of Homomorphic Encryption

Homomorphic encryption is a groundbreaking cryptographic technique that enables computations on encrypted data without the need for decryption. This eliminates the need to decrypt sensitive information before processing, significantly improving data privacy and security. Here's how homomorphic encryption can radically improve data security:

- **Enhanced Cloud Security:** Homomorphic encryption would enable secure cloud computing by allowing computations on sensitive data stored in the cloud while maintaining confidentiality. This can open up new opportunities for data analysis and collaboration while protecting data privacy.

193

- **Improved Medical Research:** Homomorphic encryption can help researchers conduct secure medical research by allowing them to analyze encrypted patient data without revealing individual identities. This can hasten medical research and development while safeguarding patient privacy.

- **Advanced Secure Search:** Imagine searching encrypted data for specific information without having to decrypt the entire data set. Homomorphic encryption can enable secure search capabilities, allowing authorized users to retrieve pertinent information from encrypted databases.

Because of the computational complexities, homomorphic encryption is still in its early stages of adoption. However, advancements in this field have enormous potential for protecting sensitive data in the future.

18.3.2 The Rise of AI-Powered Threat Detection and Response

AI is rapidly changing the cybersecurity landscape. AI-powered security solutions are becoming more sophisticated, with real-time threat detection, automated incident response, and advanced threat analysis capabilities. Here's how AI can revolutionize cybersecurity:

- **Automated Threat Detection and Analysis:** AI-powered systems can analyze massive amounts of network traffic and security data to detect anomalies and suspicious activity in real time. This can significantly improve an organization's ability to detect threats before they cause major breaches.

- **Enhanced Incident Response:** AI can automate routine incident response tasks like threat containment, evidence collection, and initial remediation. This enables security professionals to concentrate on more complex tasks and speeds up the overall incident response process.

- **Predictive Security:** Artificial intelligence systems can predict potential security vulnerabilities and recommend proactive mitigation strategies by learning from previous attacks and analyzing threat intelligence. This can help organizations stay ahead of attackers and prevent cyberattacks before they happen.

The effective integration of AI into security solutions necessitates careful consideration of ethical implications and possible biases. However, responsible development and deployment of AI-powered security tools holds significant promise for future cyber defense.

CHAPTER 19

Conclusion

Throughout this book, we have covered a wide range of security and privacy strategies that are critical for protecting modern networks. We discussed the fundamental principles of network security, the ever-present threats in the cyber landscape, and cryptography's critical role in protecting sensitive information. We then investigated various defense mechanisms, such as intrusion detection, secure network architectures, and strong perimeter defenses in protecting sensitive data. We then investigated various defense mechanisms, such as intrusion detection, secure network architectures, and strong perimeter defense.

As we investigated cloud computing and virtualization, we talked about the unique security challenges these technologies present. We emphasized the importance of securing endpoints and mobile devices, recognizing the growing reliance on these technologies in today's globalized world. The growing importance of artificial intelligence (AI) in cybersecurity was also discussed, emphasizing its potential to improve threat detection and incident response.

19.1 Synthesis of Essential Security and Privacy Strategies

The intricate dance between security and privacy is the foundation of a secure network. Throughout this book, we've looked at a wide range

© The Editor(s) (if applicable) and The Author(s), under exclusive license to APress Media, LLC, part of Springer Nature 2024
S. Lekkala and P. Gurijala, *Security and Privacy for Modern Networks*,
https://doi.org/10.1007/979-8-8688-0823-4_19

of strategies that, when combined, form a comprehensive security and privacy posture. Here's a synthesis of these key strategies:

- **Core Security Principles:** Understanding the fundamentals of network security is the first step toward laying a solid foundation. This includes implementing strong authentication mechanisms, following secure coding practices, and maintaining a layered defense strategy.

- **Threat Landscape Navigation:** Recognizing the pervasive threats in the cyber landscape is critical. This includes understanding various attack vectors, profiling threat actors, and continuously assessing network vulnerabilities.

- **Cryptography As a Cornerstone:** Encryption is the cornerstone of secure communication. You can protect sensitive information and maintain data confidentiality by implementing strong encryption algorithms and effective key management practices.

- **Defense Mechanisms:** Implementing layered defense improves your overall security posture. This includes implementing intrusion detection and prevention systems, creating secure network architectures with segmentation, and establishing strong perimeter defenses such as firewalls.

- **Endpoint and Mobile Security:** In today's mobile world, protecting endpoints and mobile devices is critical. This includes deploying endpoint protection software, putting in place endpoint detection and response (EDR) systems, and educating users about mobile security best practices.

- **Evolving with Technology:** The cybersecurity landscape is constantly changing as new technologies emerge. Maintaining a future-proof security strategy requires staying informed about advancements such as the Internet of Things (IoT) and quantum computing, as well as proactively addressing their security implications.

- **The Power of AI and Machine Learning:** AI and machine learning present promising advances in cybersecurity. Using them for threat detection, data analysis, and automated incident response can significantly boost your security posture. However, responsible development and deployment with an emphasis on ethical considerations is critical. AI and machine learning present promising advances in cybersecurity. Using them for threat detection, data analysis, and automated incident response can significantly boost your security posture. However, responsible development and deployment with an emphasis on ethical considerations is critical.

19.1.1 Synergy Is Key

Remember that these strategies work best together. A comprehensive security and privacy plan that incorporates these components can strengthen your organization's digital environment. By constantly learning, adapting, and collaborating, we can stay ahead of changing threats and create a more secure future for our networks.

19.2 Reflecting on the Progress of Network Communication Security: A Long Road, Well-Traveled

Since the early days of the Internet, network communication security has evolved dramatically. Back then, rudimentary security measures and a lack of understanding of cyber threats made networks vulnerable. Let's consider some key milestones that have significantly improved the security landscape:

- **Standardization of Protocols:** The development and adoption of standardized security protocols such as HTTPS and SSH paved the way for secure communication. These protocols encrypt data in transit, preventing eavesdropping and tampering.

- **Encryption Evolution:** Early encryption algorithms, while revolutionary at the time, have been superseded by more robust and complex alternatives. The widespread use of advanced encryption algorithms, such as AES (Advanced Encryption Standard), has significantly improved data security.

- **Security Best Practices Take Root:** The emergence of security best practices and frameworks, such as those outlined by the National Institute of Standards and Technology (NIST), has given organizations a structured approach to implementing effective security measures.

- **Rise of Security Solutions:** The cybersecurity industry has grown, with a wide range of security solutions designed to address specific threats and vulnerabilities. Organizations can access a comprehensive security toolkit, which includes firewalls, intrusion detection systems, endpoint protection software, and managed security services.

- **Increased Security Awareness:** The public's awareness of cyber threats has increased significantly. Security awareness training programs have become commonplace, teaching users how to detect phishing attempts, protect sensitive data, and engage in safe online behavior.

19.2.1 Challenges Remain

While significant progress has been made, the cybersecurity landscape remains a constant battle. New threats emerge all the time, and attackers are relentless in their pursuit of vulnerabilities. The ever-expanding attack surface, the increasing sophistication of cyberattacks, and the growing reliance on technology are all ongoing issues.

The journey to achieving robust network security is an ongoing process. However, by reflecting on our progress and recognizing the remaining challenges, we can remain motivated and committed to creating a more secure future for our interconnected world.

19.3 Future Outlook: Evolving Cybersecurity Paradigms

The future of cybersecurity is a changing landscape shaped by ongoing technological advancements. As we embrace emerging technologies, completely new paradigms for protecting our digital infrastructure will emerge. Here's a look at what the future holds:

- **The Ascendancy of the Internet of Things (IoT):** The proliferation of Internet-connected devices, ranging from smart homes to industrial control systems, results in a massive and expanding attack surface. Securing these devices will necessitate innovative solutions, such as secure-by-design principles integrated throughout the IoT device development lifecycle.

- **The Quantum Computing Challenge:** The potential for quantum computers to break widely used encryption algorithms is a serious threat. The development and implementation of Post-Quantum Cryptography (PQC) standards will be critical for data security in the quantum age.

- **Artificial Intelligence in Security Operations:** Artificial intelligence will play an increasingly important role in cybersecurity. AI-powered systems can analyze massive amounts of data to detect anomalies, predict future attacks, and automate incident response procedures. However, ethical concerns over bias and transparency in AI algorithms must be addressed.

- **The Evolving Threat Landscape:** Attackers will continue to create sophisticated techniques for exploiting vulnerabilities. Zero-day attacks on previously unknown vulnerabilities, as well as social engineering tactics that rely on advanced psychological manipulation, are just a few examples of potential threats.

- **Focus on Resilience and Continuous Improvement:** Security will shift away from a purely preventive approach and toward resilience. Organizations will need to develop systems for effectively detecting, containing, and recovering from attacks. Continuous security monitoring, vulnerability management, and periodic security assessments will be critical.

19.3.1 A Collaborative Effort

The future of cybersecurity requires a collaborative approach. Governments, industry leaders, security professionals, and individual users all play important roles. Sharing knowledge, promoting open communication, and developing international security standards are critical for creating a more secure digital ecosystem.

19.3.2 The Road Ahead

The future of cybersecurity is both daunting and exciting. We can create a more secure digital future for future generations by responsibly embracing new technologies, staying informed about evolving threats, and cultivating a security-conscious culture. Continuous learning and the development of innovative security solutions will be the cornerstones of success in the ongoing battle against cyber threats.

CHAPTER 20

Additional Resources for Continued Learning

The constantly changing cybersecurity landscape necessitates ongoing learning and professional development. This chapter lays out a strategy for expanding your knowledge and staying up to date on the latest developments in the field.

20.1 Recommended Books and Scholarly Publications

The cybersecurity field is replete with valuable resources for expanding your knowledge and staying current on emerging threats and advancements. Here is a curated list of suggested books and scholarly publications that complement the topics covered in this book:

Cryptography Foundations

- ***Cryptography Engineering: Design Principles and Practical Applications* by Niels Ferguson, Bruce Schneier, and Tadayoshi Kohno:** This comprehensive tome delves deeply into the cryptographic concepts that underpin secure communication. It looks at

S. Lekkala and P. Gurijala, *Security and Privacy for Modern Networks*, https://doi.org/10.1007/979-8-8688-0823-4_20

various encryption algorithms, key management strategies, and their practical applications in network security.

Hands-On Learning

- ***The Web Application Hacker's Handbook: Finding and Exploiting Security Flaws* by Dafydd Stuttard and Marcus Pinto:** This book has several hands-on exercises and practical examples that are great resources for understanding network security in the context of web technologies.

Best Practices and Frameworks

- **"The CIS Controls: A Framework for Effective Cybersecurity" by the Center for Internet Security (CIS):** The CIS Critical Security Controls is a set of best practices developed by a global community of cybersecurity experts. These controls provide prioritized and actionable guidance that organizations can use to strengthen their cybersecurity posture.

Attacker Mindset

- ***Hacking: The Art of Exploitation* by Jon Erickson:** This classic text provides insight into the mind of an attacker. It investigates attacker techniques for exploiting vulnerabilities and gaining unauthorized access to systems. Understanding these methods is critical for developing strong defenses.

Staying Informed

- **Industry Publications:** Keeping up with the latest threats and trends is critical. Consider subscribing to reputable cybersecurity publications and research reports from companies like Gartner, Forrester, and the SANS Institute. These resources provide valuable information about the changing threat landscape and emerging security solutions.

Remember that this list is just a starting point. The cybersecurity field is constantly evolving, so don't be afraid to look into other publications that pique your interest.

20.2 Professional Development Through Online Courses and Certifications

The cybersecurity landscape is dynamic, necessitating ongoing learning and skill development. This section highlights useful resources for expanding your knowledge and obtaining recognized credentials via online courses and certifications.

20.2.1 Enhancing Your Skillset

- **SANS Institute:** SANS, a cybersecurity training leader, provides a wide range of online courses and certifications to suit a variety of skill levels. Their course catalog includes a wide range of topics, from fundamental security principles to advanced penetration testing and incident response.

- **Industry Certifications:** Earning industry-recognized certifications validates your cybersecurity knowledge and elevates your professional standing. Consider seeking credentials such as:

  - **Certified Information Systems Security Professional (CISSP):** This globally recognized certification demonstrates a comprehensive understanding of information security principles and best practices.

  - **Certified Ethical Hacker (CEH):** This certification validates your knowledge of ethical hacking techniques, allowing you to detect and exploit vulnerabilities in a legal and controlled environment.

- **Online Learning Platforms:** Several online platforms provide high-quality cybersecurity courses created by industry professionals and top universities. Here are a few popular choices:

  - **Coursera, Udemy, and edX:** These platforms offer a vast library of cybersecurity courses, allowing you to specialize in specific areas of interest such as cloud security, mobile security, and security analytics.

  - **Vendor-Specific Certifications:** Many security software vendors provide training and certification programs specific to their products. Earning these certifications demonstrates your proficiency in using specific security solutions and can boost your marketability.

20.2.2 Choosing the Right Path

The best online courses and certifications for you will be determined by your current skillset and career goals. Here are some things to consider:

- **Your Experience Level:** Are you new to cybersecurity or want to specialize in a specific area? Choose courses that match your experience and knowledge gaps.

- **Learning Style:** Do you prefer self-paced learning modules, interactive labs, or instructor-led video lectures? Most online platforms cater to a variety of learning styles.

- **Career Aspirations:** Determine your desired career path in cybersecurity and select courses and certifications that align with those objectives.

By carefully considering these factors, you can make the most of your online learning experience and position yourself for success in the cybersecurity industry.

20.3 Key Websites and Organizations in the Cybersecurity Industry

The cybersecurity industry is a collaborative ecosystem in which knowledge sharing and collective action are critical to protecting against ever-changing threats. Here's a list of key websites and organizations that provide useful resources, share threat intelligence, and promote best practices:

- **National Institute of Standards and Technology (NIST) Cybersecurity Framework (**`www.nist.gov/cyberframework`**):** This US government agency provides a structured framework to assist organizations of all sizes in identifying, protecting against, detecting, responding to, and recovering from cyberattacks. The NIST Cybersecurity Framework outlines a prioritized approach to cybersecurity risk management.

- **Open Web Application Security Project (OWASP)** (`https://owasp.org/`): This nonprofit organization is a global community of security professionals working to improve the security of web applications. OWASP offers a wealth of free resources, such as testing guides, cheat sheets, and best practices documents, to assist developers in writing secure code and identifying vulnerabilities in web applications.

- **Cloud Security Alliance (CSA)** (`https://cloudsecurityalliance.org/`): The Cloud Security Alliance is a leading industry consortium that promotes the use of best practices in cloud security. They provide a variety of resources to help organizations secure their cloud deployments, such as cloud security guidance documents, training programs, and certification schemes.

- **CERT Coordination Center** (`www.sei.cmu.edu/about/divisions/cert/`): Carnegie Mellon University established the CERT Coordination Center, which is a reliable resource for responding to cybersecurity incidents. They offer cybersecurity incident response services, issue security advisories to alert organizations to emerging threats, and work with stakeholders to improve the overall cybersecurity posture.

- **Industry News Websites:** Follow reputable industry news websites to stay up to date on the most recent cybersecurity news, vulnerabilities, and emerging threats. Here's some suggestions:

  - **SecurityWeek** (`www.securityweek.com/`)

  - **SC Magazine** (`www.scmagazine.com/`)

  - **Krebs on Security** (`https://krebsonsecurity.com/`)

These websites feature insightful articles, security breach reports, and expert analysis of current cybersecurity trends. Following them allows you to stay informed and make proactive security decisions.

Remember that this isn't an exhaustive list. The cybersecurity industry is full of valuable resources. Consider these websites and organizations as starting points for your ongoing learning journey. By staying informed and involved in the cybersecurity community, you can help to create a more secure digital future.

Glossary of Key Terms

These websites feature insightful articles, security breach reports, and expert analysis of current cybersecurity trends. Following them allows you to stay informed and make proactive security decisions.

A.1 Comprehensive List of Security and Privacy Terminology

The ever-increasing complexity of cybersecurity necessitates a solid foundation in basic terminology. This section serves as a reference guide, with clear definitions for key security and privacy terms used throughout the book.

1. **Access Control:** The process of determining which users or systems have access to specific resources and what actions are permitted (read, write, modify, delete).

2. **Advanced Encryption Standards (AES):** A popular symmetric key encryption algorithm that is considered the industry standard for secure data encryption. AES is used for a variety of purposes, including secure communication protocols, file encryption, and disk encryption.

S. Lekkala and P. Gurijala, *Security and Privacy for Modern Networks*,
https://doi.org/10.1007/979-8-8688-0823-4

3. **Authentication**: The process of verifying a user's claimed identity prior to providing access to a system or resource. Passwords, biometrics (fingerprint scanning, facial recognition), and multifactor authentication (MFA) are all commonly used authentication methods.

4. **Authorization**: The process of determining what actions a verified user may perform within a system. Authorization controls specify a user's level of access (read-only, edit, or delete) to specific data or functionalities.

5. **Availability**: One of the most important principles of information security is ensuring that authorized users have timely and reliable access to information and systems.

6. **Biometrics**: Technologies that use unique biological characteristics like fingerprints, facial features, iris patterns, and voice patterns to identify and authenticate users.

7. **Blackhole Routing**: A security technique in which suspicious or malicious traffic is directed to a null route, effectively dropping the traffic and preventing it from reaching its intended destination.

8. **Blockchain**: A distributed ledger technology that records transactions on multiple computers connected via a network. Blockchain is known for its immutability and transparency, making it an attractive technology for cybersecurity applications.

9. **Botnet**: A network of compromised computers controlled by an attacker, commonly used to launch coordinated attacks such as denial-of-service (DoS).

10. **CIA**: The CIA Triad is a security model that represents the three key principles of information security: confidentiality, integrity, and availability.

11. **Cloud Security**: The set of practices and technologies used to protect data, applications, and infrastructure in a cloud computing environment.

12. **Cloud Security Alliance (CSA)**: A leading industry consortium that promotes best practices in cloud security. CSA provides a variety of resources and certifications to help organizations secure their cloud deployments.

13. **Cryptography**: The science of securing information through encryption and decryption. Using a cryptographic key, plain text data is encrypted and rendered unreadable. Only authorized users with the appropriate decryption key can unlock and access the original data.

14. **Cybersecurity Framework**: A set of guidelines, standards, and best practices designed to assist organizations in managing cybersecurity risks. The National Institute of Standards and Technology (NIST) Cybersecurity Framework is a well-known framework used by organizations of all sizes.

15. **Data Breach**: An unauthorized access and disclosure of sensitive, protected, or confidential data.

16. **Data Encryption**: The process of converting plain text data to an unreadable format using a cryptographic key. Encryption protects sensitive data during storage or transmission over networks.

17. **Data Encryption Standard (DES)**: A previously widely used symmetric key encryption algorithm that has been replaced by AES (Advanced Encryption Standard) due to key length limitations.

18. **Data Integrity**: Ensuring that data remains accurate and complete throughout its lifecycle, without being altered or tampered with.

19. **Data Loss Prevention (DLP)**: Technologies and policies that prevent sensitive information from being accidentally or intentionally leaked or transferred outside of an organization.

20. **Dark Web**: A portion of the Internet that is not indexed by search engines and requires specialized software to access. The dark web is frequently used for illegal activities, but it can also be used for legitimate reasons, such as anonymous communication.

21. **Demilitarized Zone (DMZ)**: A subnetwork within a local area network (LAN) that allows for a controlled connection to an external network, such as the Internet. The DMZ serves as a buffer zone, protecting the internal network from unauthorized access attempts coming from the outside network.

22. **Denial-of-Service (DoS) Attack**: An attack designed to disrupt or overwhelm a system, rendering it inaccessible to legitimate users. DoS attacks usually flood a system with too much traffic, causing it to crash or become unresponsive.

23. **Digital Certificate**: An electronic document that verifies an entity's identity (user, website, or server) and allows for secure Internet communication. Digital certificates are issued by reputable certification authorities (CAs).

24. **Digital Rights Management (DRM)**: A set of technologies that govern access and use of digital media and devices. DRM can be controversial because it limits users' fair use rights.

25. **Digital Signature**: A mathematical technique for ensuring the authenticity and integrity of a message or document. A digital signature is created with a private key and verified with the corresponding public key, ensuring that the message came from a reliable source and was not altered in transit.

26. **Distributed Denial-of-Service (DDoS) Attack**: A DoS attack launched by multiple compromised computers (bots) distributed around the world, making it more difficult to detect and mitigate than a traditional DoS attack.

27. **Encryption Algorithm**: A set of mathematical instructions for encrypting and decrypting data. Common encryption algorithms include AES (Advanced Encryption Standard), RSA (Rivest-Shamir-Adleman), and hashing algorithms such as SHA-256.

28. **Endpoint Security**: The security measures in place to protect individual networked devices (laptops, desktops, and mobile devices) from cyberattacks. Typical endpoint security solutions include antivirus software, intrusion detection/prevention systems (IDS/IPS), and endpoint detection and response (EDR) tools.

29. **Ethical Hacking**: The authorized practice of simulating cyberattacks in order to identify vulnerabilities in a computer system or network. Ethical hackers, also known as white hat hackers, help organizations improve their security posture by identifying flaws before malicious actors exploit them.

30. **Exploit**: A code snippet or a series of steps that exploits a system vulnerability. Attackers employ exploits to gain unauthorized access to a system, steal data, or disrupt operations.

31. **Firewall:** A security device that monitors incoming and outgoing network traffic and filters it according to predefined security rules. Firewalls prevent malicious traffic while allowing legitimate traffic to pass through.

32. **Firewall Rule**: A rule that specifies which types of network traffic a firewall will allow or deny. Firewall rules are established using criteria such as source and destination IP addresses, ports, and protocols.

33. **Hashing**: A cryptographic technique for converting data of any size into a fixed-length string of characters (hash value). Hashing is commonly used to verify data integrity because any change to the original data produces a different hash value.

34. **Honeynet**: A decoy network designed to entice attackers and track their activities. Honeynets aid security teams in comprehending attacker tactics and techniques.

35. **Incident Response**: The detection, analysis, containment, and recovery of a security incident. A well-defined incident response plan is critical for mitigating the damage caused by a security breach.

36. **Information Security Policy**: A document outlining an organization's security policies and procedures. Information security policies help ensure that all employees understand their security responsibilities.

37. **Intrusion Detection System (IDS)**: A system that constantly monitors network traffic and system activity for indicators of suspicious or malicious behavior. IDS systems can detect potential threats such as unauthorized access or malware infections.

38. **Intrusion Detection System (IDS) Signature**: The pattern that an IDS uses to detect malicious activity. IDS signatures are designed to detect known attack patterns.

39. **Intrusion Prevention System (IPS):** An IDS with more advanced features. In addition to detection, intrusion prevention systems actively block malicious traffic or activity.

40. **Kerberos**: A network authentication protocol that securely authenticates network users and services by relying on a central trusted authority.

41. **Key Management**: The process of creating, distributing, storing, using, rotating, and revoking cryptographic keys. Secure key management is critical to the effectiveness of encryption techniques.

42. **Least Privilege**: A security principle that states that users should only be given the bare minimum of access permissions required to complete their tasks. This principle limits the potential damage if a user account is compromised.

43. **Logic Bomb**: A type of malware that is programmed to be activated by a particular event or condition. When a logic bomb detonates, it can cause significant system damage.

44. **Malware**: Malicious software that includes viruses, worms, Trojan horses, ransomware, and spyware. Malware is intended to disrupt, damage, or steal data from a computer system.

45. **Man-in-the-Middle (MitM) Attack**: An attack in which an attacker intercepts communication between two parties and eavesdrops or modifies the messages exchanged.

46. **Multifactor Authentication (MFA)**: A method of authentication in which two or more verification factors are required to gain access to a system. Passwords, one-time codes generated by an authenticator app, fingerprint scans, and facial recognition are all common methods of multifactor authentication.

47. **Multifactor Authentication (MFA) Push Notification**: A type of MFA in which a verification code is delivered to a user's mobile device via push notification.

48. **Network Address Translation (NAT)**: A method of converting private IP addresses on a local area network (LAN) into a single public IP address for Internet access. NAT conserves public IP addresses and improves network security.

49. **Network Segmentation**: The process of dividing a network into smaller subnetworks in order to contain the spread of a security breach. A breach's impact can be mitigated by isolating critical systems and resources into separate segments.

50. **Open Source Security**: The practice of incorporating security best practices into the creation and maintenance of open source software. Open source security is critical to ensuring the reliability of widely used software applications.

51. **Open Web Application Security Project (OWASP)**: A nonprofit organization that offers free resources and best practices for secure web applications. OWASP assists developers in detecting and mitigating vulnerabilities in web applications.

52. **Password Hashing**: The process of converting a password to a fixed-length string of characters using a one-way hash function. Password hashing is a more secure option than storing passwords in plain text.

53. **Patch Management**: The process of identifying, acquiring, testing, and deploying security patches to address software and operating system vulnerabilities. Patches must be applied on time to ensure system security.

54. **Penetration Testing**: A simulated cyberattack carried out by authorized security professionals to uncover flaws in a computer system or network. Penetration testing assists organizations in determining their security posture and improving their defenses.

55. **Phishing**: A social engineering attack that tricked users into disclosing sensitive information like usernames, passwords, or credit card numbers. Phishing emails or messages frequently impersonate legitimate entities in an attempt to trick users into clicking malicious links or downloading malware-laden attachments.

56. **Phishing Kit**: A collection of pre-made tools and templates for launching phishing attacks. Phishing kits are widely available online and can be purchased even by inexperienced attackers.

57. **Physical Security**: The steps taken to prevent unauthorized access to computer systems, data centers, and other IT infrastructure. Physical security measures include access control systems, surveillance cameras, and security personnel.

58. **Phishing Simulation**: A controlled phishing attack conducted on employees to assess their awareness of phishing scams. Phishing simulations can help organizations identify employees who are vulnerable to phishing attacks and provide them with security awareness training.

59. **Public Key Infrastructure (PKI)**: A method of securely managing digital certificates used for authentication and encryption. PKI creates a trust framework in which digital certificates issued by a trusted authority verify the identity of an entity (user, website, server).

60. **Ransomware**: A type of malware that encrypts a victim's files, making them inaccessible. The attackers then demand a ransom payment in exchange for the decryption key.

61. **Ransomware Attack**: A cyberattack in which the attacker encrypts the victim's files and demands a ransom payment in exchange for the decryption key. Ransomware attacks can be extremely disruptive and costly to businesses and individuals.

62. **Reverse Engineering**: The process of analyzing a software program to determine how it functions. Reverse engineering can be used for both legitimate and malicious purposes, such as security research and exploit development.

63. **Risk Assessment**: The process of identifying, evaluating, and prioritizing an organization's security risks. Risk assessments assist organizations in allocating resources efficiently to address the most significant threats.

64. **Risk Management**: A systematic method for identifying, assessing, prioritizing, and mitigating security risks. Risk management entails putting in place appropriate controls to reduce the likelihood and severity of potential security incidents.

65. **Rootkit**: A malicious software program intended to gain unauthorized administrative access to a computer system while remaining undetected. Rootkits can be used to steal data, install additional malware, or cause system disruptions.

66. **Security Awareness Training**: Educational programs that teach users best practices for cybersecurity and how to identify and avoid cyber threats. Security awareness training is critical for lowering the likelihood of human error-related security incidents.

67. **Security Information and Event Management (SIEM)**: A system for gathering, aggregating, and analyzing security events from multiple sources across a network. SIEM enables security teams to detect and respond to security incidents more effectively.

68. **Secure Shell (SSH)**: A secure protocol that allows remote login and command-line execution over unsecured networks. SSH encrypts communication between the client and server, preventing eavesdropping and tampering.

69. **Security Operations Center (SOC)**: A centralized location where security professionals monitor and analyze security events, investigate security incidents, and take preventative measures.

70. **Security Patch**: A software update that fixes a known vulnerability in a system. Security patches are critical for system security and should be applied as soon as they are released.

71. **Social Engineering**: The practice of coercing others into taking actions or disclosing sensitive information. Social engineering attacks take advantage of human psychology and frequently involve deception or creating a false sense of urgency in order to trick users into compromising security.

72. **Social Engineering Attack**: A cyberattack technique that uses human psychology to trick users into disclosing sensitive information or performing actions that jeopardize security. Social engineering attacks can be extremely effective because they exploit human trust and emotions.

73. **Spear Phishing**: A phishing attack that aims to deceive a specific person or organization. Spear phishing attacks are frequently more successful than traditional phishing attacks due to their perceived credibility.

74. **Spoofing**: A cyberattack technique in which an attacker impersonates a legitimate user, computer, or website to gain unauthorized access to a system or network.

75. **SSL/TLS**: Encryption protocols that protect communication between a web browser and a web server. SSL/TLS encrypts data in transit, preventing eavesdropping and tampering.

76. **Supply Chain Attack**: A cyberattack directed at a company's vendors or suppliers in order to gain access to the company's systems or data. Supply chain attacks are becoming more common as attackers identify vulnerabilities in third-party relationships.

77. **Threat Actor**: A person or organization that poses a cybersecurity threat. Threat actors may be motivated by financial gain, espionage, activism, or simply causing disruption.

78. **Threat Intelligence**: The gathering, analysis, and dissemination of information about cyber threats. Threat intelligence enables organizations to better understand the changing threat landscape and make informed security decisions.

79. **Trojan Horse**: A type of malware that disguises itself as a legitimate program in order to trick users into installing it on their computers. Trojan horses, once installed, can steal data, install additional malware, or cause system disruptions.

80. **Two-Factor Authentication (2FA)**: An earlier term for Multifactor Authentication (MFA).

81. **User Access Control (UAC)**: A security feature that prevents unauthorized users from changing critical system settings or installing software. UAC prompts users for confirmation before allowing them to take actions that could harm the system.

82. **Virtual Private Network (VPN)**: An encrypted tunnel that connects a user's device to a remote server. VPNs are commonly used to provide secure remote access to a corporate network or to hide Internet browsing activity.

83. **Virus**: A type of malware capable of replicating itself and spreading from one computer to another. Viruses can damage files and steal.

84. **Vulnerability**: A weakness or flaw in a system, application, or network that attackers can use to gain unauthorized access, disrupt operations, and steal data.

85. **Vulnerability Assessment**: The process of detecting, assessing, and prioritizing vulnerabilities in a computer system or network. Vulnerability assessments help organizations understand their security posture and address potential flaws.

86. **Vulnerability Management**: The process of detecting, categorizing, prioritizing, and resolving vulnerabilities in computer systems and networks. Vulnerability management is a continuous process that is critical to maintaining a strong security posture.

87. **Web Application Firewall (WAF)**: A security device that monitors and filters HTTP traffic from a web server to the Internet. WAFs help to protect web applications from common attacks like SQL injection and cross-site scripting (XSS).

88. **Worm**: A type of malware that can replicate itself and spread throughout a network without user intervention. Worms can consume network resources and cause system disruptions.

89. **Zero-Day Attack**: A cyberattack that exploits a previously unknown vulnerability in software or systems. Zero-day attacks are especially dangerous because no patch exists to address the vulnerability.

90. **Zero-Trust Security**: A security model which assumes that no user or device is inherently trustworthy. Zero-trust security necessitates continuous authentication of all users and devices attempting to access a system or resource.

A.2 Clarifying Technical Concepts and Network Protocols

Delving into the realm of cybersecurity necessitates a solid grasp of technical concepts and network protocols. This section functions as a glossary, offering lucid explanations for these fundamental building blocks of secure communication and network operations.

- **Client-Server Model**: It is a network architecture in which client devices (such as laptops and smartphones) request resources or services from server systems that provide and manage those resources.

- **Cryptography**: It is the science of securing information through encryption and decryption techniques. Using a cryptographic key, plain text data is encrypted and rendered unreadable. Only authorized users with the appropriate decryption key can unlock and access the original data.

- **Datagram**: A self-contained unit for data transmission over a network. Each datagram contains the source and destination addresses, as well as the data payload.

- **Encryption**: It is the process of converting plain text data to an unreadable format using a cryptographic key. Encryption protects sensitive data during storage or transmission over networks.

- **IP Address**: Each device connected to an Internet Protocol (IP) network is assigned a unique numerical label that allows for communication and device identification.

- **Network Protocol**: A set of rules and specifications that govern how data is formatted, transmitted, and received across a network. Common network protocols include TCP/IP (Transmission Control Protocol/ Internet Protocol), HTTP (Hypertext Transfer Protocol), and HTTPS.

- **Packet**: A packet is a unit of data transmission in a packet switching network. Packets contain both header information (source and destination addresses) and data payload. Packet-switching networks divide large data streams into packets to ensure efficient transmission.

- **Port**: A port is a virtual communication channel on a network device (such as a server or router) that is designated for specific services or applications. Different ports handle different types of traffic (e.g., port 80 for HTTP and port 443 for HTTPS).

- **PKI**: Public Key Infrastructure (PKI) is a system that securely manages digital certificates used for authentication and encryption. PKI creates a trust framework in which digital certificates issued by a trusted authority verify the identity of an entity (user, website, server).

- **SSL**: Secure Sockets Layer (SSL) and Transport Layer Security (TLS) are encryption protocols that ensure secure communication between a web browser and a web server. SSL/TLS encrypts data in transit, preventing eavesdropping and tampering.

- **Session**: A session is a temporary communication link established between two networked devices to exchange data. Sessions have a defined beginning and end point.

- **Symmetric Encryption**: It is a method of encrypting and decrypting data using the same secret key.

- **TCP/IP**: Transmission Control Protocol/Internet Protocol is a set of communication protocols that serve as the foundation for the Internet. TCP ensures consistent data delivery by breaking it down into packets, acknowledging receipt, and retransmitting lost packets. IP addresses packets and routes them across networks.

- **UDP**: User Datagram Protocol is a connectionless protocol for datagram transmission. UDP prioritizes speed over reliability, making it ideal for real-time applications such as online gaming or video streaming, where occasional packet loss is acceptable.

- **VPN**: A virtual private network (VPN) is a secure tunnel that encrypts data traffic between the user's device and a remote server. VPNs are commonly used to provide secure remote access to a corporate network or to hide Internet browsing activity.

By understanding these technical concepts and network protocols, you'll be better able to navigate the complexities of cybersecurity and make informed decisions about protecting your systems and data. Remember that this is a foundational list, and further exploration of these concepts is encouraged for a more in-depth understanding.

Index

A

ABAC, *see* Attribute-Based Access
    Control (ABAC)
ABE, *see* Attribute-Based
    Encryption (ABE)
Access control lists (ACLs), 51
Access control models, 52
    identity management, 53
    methods, 54
    optimization, 54
    streamlining identity
        management, 53
ACLs, *see* Access control
    lists (ACLs)
Advanced Encryption Standard
    (AES), 41, 69, 200, 213
AES, *see* Advanced Encryption
    Standard (AES)
AI, *see* Artificial intelligence (AI)
Anomaly-based detection
    methods, 100
Artificial intelligence (AI), 74, 129,
    167, 197, 199
    accountability, 174
    AI-powered security
        solutions, 175

    bias/fairness, 173
    comprehensive approach,
        177, 178
    cybersecurity, 202
    data security, 176
    ethical implication, 173
    human in the loop security, 175
    ML (*see* Machine learning (ML))
    phishing emails, 176
    privacy concerns/data
        security, 174
    social engineering, 176
    strong password habits, 176
    threat detection
        analysis/prioritization, 169
        capabilities, 167
        challenges/
          considerations, 169
        continuous learning/
          adaptation, 169
        unique capabilities, 168
    transparency/explainability, 173
    user awareness training
        programs, 176, 178, 179
Attribute-Based Access Control
    (ABAC), 52

X, Y

Z

Printed in the United States
by Baker & Taylor Publisher Services